Christine House
John Stevens

Grammar no problem

Eine Englischgrammatik mit Übungen

Cornelsen

Grammar – no problem
Eine Englischgrammatik mit Übungen

Verfasser
Christine House
John Stevens

Berater
Holger Freese,
Professor am Staatlichen Seminar für Schulpädagogik, Freiburg

Redaktion
Helga Holtkamp

Redaktionelle Mitarbeit
Andrew Dowdall, Tom Parkinson
Barbara Swayne, Amy Klement (amerikanisches Englisch)

Design und Layout
Typoly Berlin

Danksagung
Die Autoren und der Verlag danken allen Teilnehmern in Volkshochschul- und Firmenkursen, die durch ihr unermüdliches Testen und ihre Rückmeldungen die vorliegende Grammatik mitgestaltet haben. Viele Englisch Lernende im Eins-zu-Eins Unterricht haben alle Erklärungen und Übungen mehrmals bearbeitet. Diesen Lernenden gilt unser ganz besonderer Dank, denn ihre Geduld und ihre Kritik haben dazu beigetragen, dass **Grammar – no problem** sich so gut zum eigenständigen Lernen eignet. Unser besonderer Dank gilt auch Herrn Professor Freese, dessen ausführliche Kommentare den Autoren dabei geholfen haben, sich auf das Wesentliche zu konzentrieren und die Erklärungen einfach und verständlich zu halten.

www.cornelsen.de

1. Auflage, 5. Druck 2007 / 06

Druck: CS Druck Cornelsen Stürtz, Berlin

ISBN 978-3-8109-8452-4

Inhalt gedruckt auf säurefreiem Papier aus nachhaltiger Forstwirtschaft.

Abweichende Formen im amerikanischen Englisch werden in diesem Schlüssel in Klammern angegeben, z.B. on holiday (AE: on vacation).

Exercises 1

A
1 a
2 a
3 b
4 b
5 a
6 a

B
1 I don't normally go to bed before 10 o'clock.
2 This book doesn't teach vocabulary.
3 I don't go to work by train.
4 We don't usually have an English lesson on Tuesday.
5 My sisters don't live in Manchester.
6 What time do you go to bed?
7 What does this book teach?
8 How do you go to work?
9 When do you usually have an English lesson?
10 Where do your sisters live?

C
1 lives
2 don't know
3 always work
4 don't have
5 don't smoke
6 doesn't work

D
1 No, she doesn't.
2 Yes, we do.
3 No, they don't.
4 Yes, he/she does.
5 Yes, I do.
6 No, she doesn't.

E
1 do you start
2 does Paul go
3 do they have
4 do you play
5 do you do

Exercises 2

A
1 a
2 b
3 a
4 b
5 b
6 b

B
1 I'm not working in Leipzig this week.
2 The children aren't watching Sesame Street.
3 The Pope isn't visiting Thailand at the moment.
4 We are not working from 8 till 3 this week.
5 I'm not learning English for fun.
6 Where are you working this week?
7 What are the children watching?
8 Which country is the Pope visiting?
9 When are you working this week?
10 Why are you learning English?

C
1 B: 's studying
2 B: 'm looking for
3 B: 'm working
4 A: Are you waiting
B: 'm waiting

D
1 Yes, she is.
2 Yes, I am.
3 No, it isn't.
4 Yes, we are.

E
1 is Joe studying
2 is Jane working
3 are you waiting
4 are you/we meeting

Exercises 3

A
1 a
2 a
3 b
4 a
5 a
6 a

B
1 We usually go shopping on Fridays. This week we're going on Saturday.
2 John always goes to work by car. Today he's going by bus because his car is at the garage.
3 The children sometimes visit their grandparents. This Sunday they're staying at home.
4 Jane is going to Australia for Christmas this year. She often spends Christmas abroad.
5 This week I'm not working on Friday. I never work on Mondays, so that means I can have a long weekend.

C
1 B: 's staying
A: is she staying
2 A: are you going
B: 'm going, 'm learning
A: go
3 A: Do you normally go
B: usually spend, 're staying
A: 're not going
4 A: does your brother work
B: works
A: isn't working

D
1 We're not going on holiday (AE: on vacation) this year because we're moving.
2 It's snowing a lot today. It doesn't normally/usually snow so much in March.
3 My brother speaks three languages. Now he's learning a fourth – Russian.
4 What are you doing this weekend? Are you staying at home (AE: staying home)?
5 This evening we're going to a vegetarian restaurant because our friends don't eat meat.

Cornelsen

Exercises 4

A
1 a
2 b
3 a
4 a
5 a
6 a

B
1 looks, is looking
2 see, am seeing
3 think, 'm thinking
4 are having, have

C
1 A: do you think
B: prefer
2 A: does this word mean, don't understand
B: don't know, think
3 A: doesn't seem
B: 'm seeing, 're thinking
4 A: Do you remember
B: 'm having
5 A: Do you need
B: 'm just thinking, don't think

D
1 This book doesn't belong to me. Does it belong to you?
2 I'm thinking about Ann's question. I think we need more time.
3 Do you have time this evening? – It depends on my work.
4 Why are you looking at that car? – Because it looks so great. But I think it's too expensive.
5 Is Tom still having breakfast? – No, I think he is ready. That means we can go.

Exercises 5

A
1 b
2 a
3 b
4 b
5 a
6 b

B
1 I didn't get up early yesterday.
2 This jacket wasn't expensive.
3 Sam didn't go to the USA last year.
4 Judy didn't ring Clive last week.
5 What time did you get up yesterday?
6 How much was your jacket?
7 Where did Sam go last year?
8 Who did Judy ring last week?

C
1 A: did your son give
B: forgot
2 A: did you buy
B: didn't buy, was
3 A: tried, weren't
B: stayed, felt
4 A: Did you have
B: had, didn't do
5 A: did you get
B: left, missed

D
1 did you start
2 did your coat cost
3 Did you see
4 Did you pay

E
1 No, she wasn't.
2 Yes, it did.
3 No, I wasn't.
4 Yes, I did.
5 Yes, he did.
6 No, we didn't.

Exercises 6

A
1 a
2 b
3 b
4 a
5 b
6 a

B
1 Which country was the president visiting when he became ill? – He was visiting Spain.
2 How fast were they driving when the accident happened? – They were driving at 120 km an hour.
3 What was Helen doing when she met her husband? – She was doing research for her new book.
4 Who was John speaking to when the secretary walked in? – He was speaking to his boss.
5 Where were the children playing when the dog attacked them? – They were playing in the park.

C
1 A: Was it raining, left
B: got, was shining
2 A: did you switch
B: was watching, wanted
3 A: Did you phone
B: forgot, remembered, was waiting
4 A: were you going, saw, seemed
B: was going, was wearing
5 A: gave
B: went, came, was talking

D
1 When the teacher came into the classroom, the children were playing with a ball.
2 I rang/phoned/called (AE: phoned/called) you at eleven. Where were you? – I was sitting in the garden and I didn't hear the phone.
3 Did you see Jill yesterday? – Yes, she looked terrible. She was wearing an awful green dress.
4 When we arrived in London it was raining and we wanted to go back home.
5 This time last week I was lying on the beach.

Exercises 7

A
1 a (AE: *beide Sätze möglich*)
2 b
3 b
4 b
5 b
6 a

B
1 Paul has been to the USA before.
2 Has your son ever run away from home? (AE: Did your son ever run ...)
3 I have just finished my homework. (AE: I just finished ...)
4 Have you done your homework yet? (AE: Did you do ...)
5 We have always wanted to go to Israel.
6 I have had a lot of work recently.

C
1 B: 's just heard (AE: just heard)
2 B: haven't been
3 A: have they gone out (AE: did they go out)
B: 've just missed (AE: just missed), 've gone (AE: went)
4 A: Has your husband given up
B: 's had

D
1 No, he hasn't.
2 Yes, I have.
3 No, they haven't.
4 Yes, she has.

E
1 have you invited
2 has John Grisham written
3 Have you decided
4 Have you been
5 Have you ever been

Exercises 8

A
1 a
2 a
3 a
4 b
5 b
6 b (AE: *beide Sätze möglich*)

B
1 A: Have you ever broken your arm or your leg?
B: Yes, I broke my leg three years ago.
2 A: Have you read Robert Goddard's latest book? (AE: Did you read ...)
B: Yes, I read it while I was on holiday.
3 A: Have you found your keys yet? (AE: Did you find ...)
B: Yes, I found them a few minutes ago.
4 A: Have you done your homework yet? (AE: Did you do ...)
B: Yes, I did it yesterday.

C
1 A: Have you spoken
B: phoned, rang, wasn't
2 A: Did you learn
B: was, 've forgotten, didn't like, didn't do
3 A: 've just booked (AE: just booked)
B: got, haven't decided
4 A: decided, bought, 've never worn
B: tried, wasn't, gave up

D
1 John has bought a new car. He bought it last week. It wasn't expensive.
2 You can have the book. I've read (AE: I read) it. I read it on holiday; it was very good.
3 Have you written (AE: Did you write) all the invitations? – No, I only wrote ten yesterday.
4 Has Sandra given (AE: Did Sandra give) us her new telephone number? – No. She sent us a postcard last week, but she forgot the new number.
5 Have you heard (AE: Did you hear) from Hilary and George? They've moved! (AE: They moved!) – Really? When did they move?

Exercises 9

A
1 b
2 b
3 b
4 b
5 b
6 a

B
1 since
2 for
3 since
4 since
5 since
6 for

C
1 A: Have you met
B: 've known, since, haven't seen, for
2 A: has your son been
B: Since, 's only written
3 A: haven't heard, since, Have you seen
B: 's been, haven't spoken, for
4 A: 've always wanted, Have you ever been
B: haven't had, for
5 A: have you been
B: 've been, since, 've never had

D 1 We're in Spain now. We've been here for a week.
2 I've had problems with my computer all day. I have / have got a very old computer.
3 How long has your son been in Austria? Is he in Salzburg or Vienna?
4 I've known Mary all my life. We see each other every month.
5 How long have you known your husband? – We've known each other for ages, but we've only been married for two months. We're very happy.

Exercises 10

A 1 b 2 a 3 a 4 b 5 b 6 a

B 1 haven't had 2 didn't ring 3 haven't had 4 has been 5 haven't seen

C 1 A: haven't had, had, got up
B: opened
2 A: worked, haven't had
B: made
3 A: did he die
B: was, went, died, 's been
4 A: 've decided, Have you ever been
B: took, was

D 1 It's three o'clock and I've done nothing all day. Yesterday I just sat in the garden all day.
2 Twenty years ago we read Hamlet at school and yesterday I saw the play at the theatre.
3 My husband has been in hospital (AE: in the hospital) for a week. He was in hospital (AE: in the hospital) last year too.
4 It is Tuesday and my daughter still hasn't rung/called/phoned (AE: called/phoned). She flew to Rome on Saturday and promised to ring/call/phone (AE: call/phone).

Exercises 11

A 1 b 2 b 3 a 4 b 5 a 6 b

B 1 A: How long have you been waiting?
B: For 20 minutes.
2 A: How long has your wife been learning French?
B: Since last October.
3 A: How long have your children been travelling round Europe?
B: Since the beginning of the summer holidays.
4 A: How long have you been looking for a new flat?
B: For ages.
5 A: How long has it been snowing?
B: Since I got up.

C 1 B: 's been working
2 A: have been living
B: 've been
3 A: have you been looking for
B: 've known
4 A: 've been staring
B: 've been thinking, 's been
4 A: has she been
5 A: 've been waiting
B: 've been trying
A: 've had

D 1 We live in Leipzig. We've lived / been living there for seven years.
2 Do you know Harry? – Yes, we've known each other for years.
3 I've got (AE: I have ...) a headache. I've had a headache for three days.
4 I work in the export department. How long have you been working here?
5 My husband always works hard, but recently he's been working too much.

Exercises 12

A 1 a 2 b 3 a 4 b 5 a 6 a

B 1 have taught, 've been
2 has Jenny been learning, has she had
3 has been talking, has made
4 has been washing, has washed

C 1 are building, have been building, have built
2 'm writing, 've written, have been writing
3 've cut, is cutting, 've been cutting
4 've been reading, 'm reading, 've read
5 has played, 's playing, has been playing

D 1 A: have you been doing
B: 've been helping
2 A: have you been, haven't seen
B: 've been watching
3 A: Do you like
B: 've only been, seems
4 A: 's been, have you been speaking
B: wants

Exercises 13

A 1 b 2 a 3 b 4 a

B 1 I had already done all the housework when I left home yesterday morning.
2 We had only been abroad once before we flew to China last year.
3 The little girl was upset because she had lost her mother in the supermarket.
4 Joe had almost given up when he finally found a new job.
5 Our visitors didn't arrive on time because their car broke down / had broken down on the motorway.
6 They had not been married very long when they decided to get divorced.

C 1 had
2 wrapped up
3 had bought
4 was packing
5 called
6 decided
7 hadn't seen
8 woke up
9 hadn't been
10 had been looking forward to
11 landed
12 went
13 had been waiting
14 realized
15 went
16 filled in
17 told
18 met / had met
19 took
20 were standing
21 arrived
22 were
23 got off
24 explained
25 had happened
26 were walking
27 came
28 had sent

Exercises 14

A 1 b
2 a
3 a
4 b
5 a
6 a

B 1 I have been trying to phone Sue all day.
2 We hadn't seen him since we moved.
3 Bill and Carol had so many arguments when they were travelling round Europe that they decided to come home.
4 My son is working in the local supermarket at the moment – it's a holiday job. He doesn't like the work much but he needs the money.
5 When we arrived in Manchester, the sun was shining. Obviously it had been raining because the ground was still wet.
6 I had not been looking for a new flat for very long before I found one I liked.

C 1 A: were you going, hadn't realized / didn't realize
B: were going
2 A: did Tom break
B: fell, was cleaning, had already started
3 A: were staying, had only been walking
B: started
4 A: lost, decided
B: 've been saving
5 A: wasn't listening
B: 've probably been waiting, 've ordered

D 1 Paul is learning Spanish. He has been learning it for two months. The course takes place on Mondays.
2 Have you heard (AE: Did you hear)? Tom's broken (AE: Tom broke) his leg. It happened last week when he was cleaning the windows.
3 I had been waiting for an opportunity to wash the car. I was just drying it when I saw the black clouds.
4 My wife has been looking for a new job since the beginning of the year. When she lost her job she had been working at the company for over 20 years.
5 We were late yesterday. Our friends had already been waiting for half an hour when we finally arrived.

Exercises 15

A 1 b
2 a
3 b
4 a
5 b
6 a

B 1 She will be 18.
2 My mother will probably come for Christmas.
3 If you take this bag, I'll carry the heavy suitcase.
4 The weather forecast says it will rain tomorrow.
5 I hope we won't be late.
6 I'll post your letter for you if you like.

C 1 A: want to
B: 'll
2 A: 'll
B: 'll
3 A: 'll, won't
B: 'll, 'll
4 A: want to, don't want to, 'll
B: will, 'll
5 A: want to, will
B: 'll

D 1 Have you got / Do you have an umbrella? I'm sure you'll need one later.
2 Jill wants more money. I think she'll look for a new job soon.
3 Don't forget to buy stamps. – No, I won't forget!
4 What film (AE: movie) do you want to see?
5 I'll help you later. This afternoon I want to buy a birthday present for my aunt. When I'm back, I'll call/ring/phone (AE: call/phone) you.

Exercises 16

A 1 b
2 b
3 a
4 a
5 b
6 b

B 1 I'm meeting a friend after work tomorrow.
2 Does Jane's train arrive at 11.30 or 12.30?
3 We're not having a holiday this summer. We're staying here.
4 Here is a list of people we're inviting to our wedding.
5 The concert starts at 8 o'clock.
6 What are you doing this weekend?

C 1 B: 's not going to apply, 's going to travel
2 A: 'll give
B: 'll ring
3 A: 're going to be
B: won't think
4 A: 's going to buy
B: 'll show
5 A: 'm going to throw
B: 'll take

D 1 Be careful! The vase is going to fall over.
2 I'll drive you if you want. – Thanks, but it's all organized. We're taking / going to take a taxi (AE: cab).
3 When does the film (AE: movie) start?
4 Our boss is getting married next week. We're going to buy him an apron as a wedding present.
5 I'm going for a walk. – Good idea. I'll come with you.

Exercises 17

A 1 a
2 a
3 a
4 b

B 1 At 12 o'clock Sam will be cooking lunch. At 1.10 we will be eating. At 2.45 I will have done the washing up.
2 At 8.30 they will be travelling to school. At 9.30 they will be sitting in their first lesson. By 10.40 they will have had two lessons.
3 This time tomorrow my cleaning woman will have started work. By 1.30 she will have finished work in my flat. At 1.30 she will be cleaning my neighbour's flat.

C 1 A: will have arrived
B: 'll phone
2 A: will win
B: 'll be sitting
3 A: 'll ring
B: 'll be eating
4 A: 'll help
B: 'll have finished

D 1 Next year my parents will have been married for 40 years.
2 This time tomorrow I'll be lying on the beach.
3 Ellen will have arrived by now. It's already after 11.00.
4 I'll have read (finished) this book by Tuesday. Then you can have it.
5 I'll call/ring/phone (AE: call/phone) tomorrow. – OK, but not between 7 and 8 o'clock because we'll be eating.

Exercises 18

A 1 a
2 a
3 b
4 b
5 b
6 a

B
1 Yes, I do.
2 Yes, they are.
3 No, he didn't.
4 Yes, they have.
5 No, she doesn't.

C
1 Do you know where the post office is, please? – No, I'm sorry, I don't.
2 Have the children done their homework yet? – Yes, they have.
3 Did you go shopping yesterday? – Yes, I did.
4 Is Sally coming tomorrow? – No, I'm afraid she isn't.
5 Has Paul ever been abroad? – No, he hasn't.

D
1 Have you seen my car keys? – No, I haven't.
2 Were you at school (AE: in school) yesterday? – Yes, I was.
3 Are you going to the cinema (AE: to a movie / the movies) this evening? – Yes, we are.
4 Can Tom swim? – No, he can't.
5 Have you got Jane's new address? – Yes, I have. / Do you have Jane's new address? – Yes, I do.

Exercises 19

A
1 a
2 b
3 b
4 a
5 a
6 a

B
1 Who does Jane share a flat with?
2 How many people came to your birthday party last week?
3 What wine goes best with beef: red or white?
4 Who helped you with your homework?
5 What normally happens at Christmas in your office?

C
1 did you go with
2 paid for the tickets
3 did you do
4 were there
5 did you sit next to
6 did you talk about

D
1 What happened last week? How did the accident happen?
2 Who called/phoned/rang (AE: called/phoned) so late yesterday?
3 Who did you go shopping with yesterday?
4 Who sent you this postcard?
5 Who did you write to when you were on holiday?

Exercises 20

A
1 a
2 a
3 b
4 a
5 b
6 a

B
1 haven't I?
2 isn't it?
3 do you?
4 don't you?
5 didn't he?
6 aren't I?

C
1 're not angry, are you?
2 's found, hasn't she?
3 are (playing), aren't they?
4 won't be, will you?
5 couldn't, could you? / can't, can you?
6 's moving, isn't he?

D
1 You're coming tomorrow, aren't you?
2 That was very expensive, wasn't it?
3 John didn't call/phone/ring (AE: call/phone) yesterday, did he?
4 You haven't lived / been living here long, have you?
5 The book's very interesting, isn't it?

Exercises 21

A
1 b
2 b
3 a
4 b
5 b
6 a

B 1 The Sydney Opera House was designed by a Danish architect.
2 The new art gallery will be opened next week by the Queen.
3 'Travelled' is spelt with one 'l' in American English.
4 Bags must not be taken into the museum.
5 A lot of people have been killed in road accidents so far this year.

C 1 What is made in this factory?
2 When will the new airport be built?
3 How long ago was the new concert hall opened?
4 How many people have been invited so far?
5 How often are elections held in Great Britain?
6 When was your car stolen?

D 1 How is this word pronounced?
2 When was this bridge built?
3 Ten people were injured in an accident yesterday.
4 A decision will be made next week.
5 Telephone cards can be bought almost everywhere.

Exercises 22

A 1 a
2 b
3 a
4 b
5 b
6 a

B 1 wasn't told about the meeting.
2 were you paid?
3 been explained to you?
4 will be shown on TV.
5 must be written this week.
6 have been asked to help at the school Christmas party.

C 1 Has David been offered a place at university yet?
2 Why was the flight cancelled yesterday?
3 When will the book be published?
4 What is being built here?
5 Who was this book written by?

D 1 Our new couch has just been delivered (AE: was just delivered).
2 Last week I was offered a job in another department.
3 Can I help you? – No, thank you. I'm being served.
4 When we arrived at the hotel, our room was (just) being cleaned.
5 At the moment everything is being done to solve the problem.

Exercises 23

A 1 b
2 b
3 a
4 b
5 a
6 a

B 1 were able to
2 haven't been able to
3 couldn't / wasn't able to
4 'll be able to
5 could / were able to

C 1 Can you speak
2 Could you swim
3 Were you able to sleep
4 Will he be able to play

D 1 Were you able to work in the garden last weekend or was the weather too bad?
2 I can see the mountains from my window.
3 I'm sorry. I haven't been able to translate your letter yet.
4 Please help me. I can't do it on my own.
5 Have you been able to speak to your boss yet?

Exercises 24

A 1 a
2 a
3 b
4 a
5 b
6 b

B 1 doesn't have to
2 mustn't
3 don't have to
4 mustn't
5 mustn't
6 doesn't have to

C 1 do we have to
2 Did you have to
3 Do you have to
4 'll have to
5 Have you had to

D 1 I really must (AE: have to) learn more grammar.
2 Did you have enough pounds on holiday or did you have to change more?
3 My doctor is good, but you always have to wait.
4 Do we have to come (with you)?
5 I don't have/need to/needn't (AE: don't have/need to) work tomorrow.

Exercises 25

A 1 b
2 b
3 a
4 a
5 a
6 b

B 1 a and b
2 b
3 a and b
4 b
5 a and b

C 1 B: may
2 B: can't
3 A: can't
B: may
4 A: may
B: may not
5 A: Can
B: can

D 1 May/Can I close the window?
2 I'm sorry, but you can't leave your bicycle here.
3 Could I call/phone/ring (AE: call/phone) back later? – Of course you can.
4 The letter could/might be from Paul – he said he'd write to me.
5 Take an umbrella. It might rain later.

Exercises 26

A 1 b
2 b
3 a
4 a
5 b
6 a

B 1 going to the theatre.
2 stealing the bike.
3 living in Australia.
4 booking early at the new Indian restaurant.
5 seeing Carol at the party.
6 going to work by car.

C 1 A: to do
B: working, to have, to speak
2 A: turning off
B: going, to watch
3 A: driving
B: getting up, to go
4 A: to use
B: to send
5 A: to go, to go
B: having, sleeping

D 1 I suggest writing a letter to the company.
2 My neighbour (AE: neighbor) offered to repair my car.
3 I can't imagine leaving this area, but my wife wants to move.
4 We would like to reserve a table. We like sitting by the window.
5 Sue and Tom (have) promised to be punctual / on time.

Exercises 27

A 1 b
2 a
3 b
4 b
5 b
6 b

B 1 to working on Saturdays.
2 in meeting your new boss.
3 against buying a new kitchen.
4 in finding a parking space.
5 on helping me.
6 to leaving so early.

C 1 A: of getting
B: to pay
2 A: at remembering, of/about booking, to come
B: going
3 A: to jogging, to having
B: to run, taking, on coming
4 A: buying
B: to get, about/of buying

D 1 We (have) bought a boat instead of going on holiday (AE: vacation).
2 Paul is against buying a new car.
3 Sue is good at explaining grammar.
4 I'm afraid of going to the dentist.
6 We look / are looking forward to seeing you next week.

Exercises 28

A 1 b
2 b
3 a
4 b
5 b
6 b

B 1 to go to the bank.
2 going to Alaska.
3 smoking?
4 to have coffee together.
5 leaving my wallet in the living room.
6 being very ill when I was ten.

C 1 A: to drive, to take
B: taking, to pass
2 A: leaving
B: leaving
3 A: to tell, to pay, to reduce
B: doing, trying
4 A: having, working
B: not having to

D 1 I must remember to go to the bank.
2 We've stopped (AE: We stopped) looking for a new flat (AE: apartment). We can't afford to move.
3 I hate having to work at weekends (AE: on the weekend).
4 Where is my dictionary? I remember lending it to Tom.

Exercises 29

A 1 b
2 a
3 b
4 a
5 a
6 b

B 1 Dave would like me to come to his party.
2 I expect everyone to be here by nine o'clock.
3 I warned the children not to play on the road.
4 Sue persuaded Jim to go to the theatre.
5 My mother let me borrow her car.
6 Jane's mother doesn't want her to hitchhike round Europe.

C 1 me to babysit
2 me to lend
3 not to park
4 me to phone
5 you do

D 1 I'm waiting for someone to repair the heating.
2 Last year I let my daughter go on holiday (AE: vacation) with a friend.
3 My wife wants me to stay at home (AE: stay home) and look after the children.
4 We warned you not to invest in this company.
5 We would like our son to do (AE: take) a language course in the school holidays (AE: during summer vacation).

Exercises 30

A 1 b
2 a
3 a
4 a

B 1 I'm not used to speaking in front of so many people.
2 I'm used to working at night.
3 I'm not used to doing that!
4 He's not used to drinking so much.
5 I did, but my wife comes from England so she's used to driving on the left.

C
1 to going
2 to work
3 to sleeping
4 to eating
5 to live

D
1 Last week I booked my first package holiday.
2 I always used to say I would never book a package holiday.
3 When I was younger I never used to book a hotel, just the flight.
4 I always used to go camping.
5 Once I stayed in a guesthouse, but it was terrible.

Exercises 31

A
1 b
2 a
3 b
4 b
5 a
6 b

B
1 ~~which~~
3 ~~which~~
4 ~~that~~
6 ~~which~~

C
1 (which/that)
2 whose
3 What
4 (which/that)
5 which/that
6 that

D
1 The man who is just going into the bank is my ex-boss.
2 The people we met at Jane's party called/phoned/rang (AE: called/phoned) yesterday evening.
3 This evening I'm meeting the friend whose husband is an actor and is often on TV.
4 I can really recommend the film (AE: movie) we saw at the weekend (AE: on the weekend).
5 What we have / have got to do is not very easy.

Exercises 32

A
1 b
2 b
3 b
4 a

B
1 ~~who~~
4 ~~who~~

C
1 you were talking to?
2 you wrote to?
3 Tom grew up in?
4 she applied for?
5 Jack told us about?

D
1 Mrs Fuchs, who always waters our plants when we're on holiday (AE: vacation), is moving.
2 The friend I was waiting for yesterday had an accident.
3 David hasn't written us a postcard, which is very unusual.
4 My boss, who comes from Brazil, got married yesterday.
5 What's the name of the hotel we stayed in last year?

Exercises 33

A
1 b
2 a
3 b
4 a

B
1 If the taxi doesn't come soon, we'll miss our train.
2 I'm sure you'll feel better if you lie down.
3 What will you do if your boss doesn't let you take time off?
4 If I don't get to the bank today, I'll change some money at the airport.
5 If you get Sarah's birthday present, I'll get the flowers for her.
6 I'll give you a lift tomorrow if your car's still at the garage.

C
1 drive, won't be able to
2 will still get, post
3 don't invite, won't come
4 buy, will probably have to
5 clean, will probably rain

D 1 If he doesn't come soon, we'll start without him.
2 What will you do if it rains at the weekend (AE: on the weekend)?
3 Will you go home early tomorrow if your boss lets you?
4 I won't buy the coat if it's not reduced.
5 If Tim doesn't win the game tomorrow, he will be very disappointed.

Exercises 34

A	1	b	3	a
	2	b	4	b

B 1 If you worked less, you'd have more time for your family.
2 If she didn't buy so many, she'd be able to afford more holidays.
3 If I were you, I'd apply for it.
4 If he was/were more punctual, he would probably get on better with his boss.
5 If they waited a couple of months, it wouldn't be so cold.

C 1 I'm sure it will never happen, but if I lost my passport, I would go to the police.
2 If you want to come with us on Saturday, I'll try to get another ticket.
3 If I were you, I'd save some money every month.
4 If I don't have time to call you this evening, I'll phone you tomorrow – I promise.
5 If we didn't have one, I'm sure we'd go on holiday more often.
6 I'll give you a lift to the airport tomorrow if your husband can't take you.

D 1 If I were you, I wouldn't go on Friday.
2 I'd help you if I was/were here at the weekend (AE: on the weekend).
3 If I didn't have to change twice, I'd go to work by bus.
4 My sister would only work part-time if she didn't need the money.
5 If my parents didn't live so far away, I'd visit them more often.

Exercises 35

A	1	a	3	b
	2	b	4	a

B 1 If we hadn't managed to get a last-minute holiday, we wouldn't have been able to go away.
2 I'm sure you would have got (AE: gotten) it if you had applied.
3 The workers wouldn't have gone on strike if the management had agreed to pay them more.
4 If he had studied harder, he might have passed.
5 Would she have taken the job if she had known?

C 1 If I had listened to the radio in the morning, I would have known about the hold-up.
2 If Sally had applied for a visa early enough, she wouldn't have had to cancel her trip.
3 If we'd had our mobile phone with us, we could have phoned to say we'd be late.
4 If I hadn't taken the risk, I wouldn't have made a lot of money.
5 If the children had known that the ice was too thin, they would/might not have gone skating.

D 1 If I hadn't had so much luggage, I would have come by bus, not by taxi (AE: cab).
2 If we'd known how full the exhibition is at weekends (AE: on the weekend), we would have waited until Monday.
3 If you hadn't called/phoned/rung (AE: called/phoned) me, I would have overslept.
4 The accident wouldn't have happened if Pete hadn't drunk so much.
5 Would you have moved if you'd known how noisy it is in this street (AE: on this street)?

Exercises 36

A	1	a	4	b
	2	b	5	b
	3	b	6	b

B 1 could help last week and said Sue might have time too
2 had bought a house in the country and they thought it would be better for the children.
3 would have to work harder if I wanted to pass the exam.
4 'd had two job interviews but he wasn't really interested in either of the jobs.

C
1 petrol would soon be much cheaper.
2 temperatures in June had been lower than in March.
3 Bill Gates had decided to give all his money to charity.
4 Prince Charles was getting married again.
5 scientists had found a cure for Aids.

D
1 you weren't hungry and you didn't want to go out for dinner.
2 you weren't interested in it.
3 you'd get white wine.
4 couldn't come, had to work.

Exercises 37

A
1 a
2 b
3 a
4 a

B
1 The driving instructor told the student to drive more slowly.
2 The doctor told the patient to stay in bed and not to smoke.
3 The old lady asked the man to help her.
4 The guide told the tourists not to forget their passports.
5 The boss asked the secretary to finish the report.

C
1 her husband was starting a new job that day.
2 they were meeting in the Red Lion the following week
3 would be there soon and that she wasn't normally late
4 they (had) moved the day before and she would let me know as soon as they had a new phone number.

D
1 if I had got a birthday card from Sue.
2 if I knew what time the concert started
3 if I could babysit for them the following Saturday.
4 where we were meeting the others that evening.
5 if he could borrow my bike the following weekend

Exercises 38

A
1 b
2 b
3 b
4 a
5 a
6 b

B
1 feels
2 wonder
3 imagine
4 enjoyed ourselves
5 hurt himself
6 concentrate

C
1 yourself
2 /
3 himself
4 each other
5 /, yourself, yourself
6 /, each other, /

D
1 I wonder when we'll arrive.
2 Paul complained yesterday – he couldn't concentrate because the neighbours (AE: neighbors) were so noisy.
3 We're meeting at eight, but I can't remember where.
4 I have lots of photos of my children, but none of myself.
5 At the weekend (AE: On the weekend) I like to lie down and relax / lying down and relaxing.

Exercises 39

A
1 a
2 b
3 b
4 b
5 b
6 a

B
1 extremely carefully.
2 well.
3 really fast.
4 regularly.
5 completely unexpectedly.

C
1 A: late, lately
B: careful, hard
A: badly, real
2 A: good
B: beautiful, hardly
A: unusual
3 A: unhappy
B: terribly, suddenly A: well
4 A: terrible, badly
B: slightly, serious
A: bad, dangerous
5 A: angry, noisy, loud, properly
B: nicely
A: noisy, late

D 1 John felt terrible. He was terribly tired.
2 He doesn't usually dream much. One evening he had an unusual dream.
3 Suddenly he heard something. A sudden noise woke him up.
4 His son and his friends were listening to loud music and talking loudly in the living room.
5 "You look very angry," his son said. "Why are you looking at me so angrily?"

Exercises 40

A 1 a
2 a
3 b
4 b
5 a
6 b

B 1 harder, than
2 as, more expensive than
3 more difficult, than
4 cheapest, best
5 more serious than
6 worst

C 1 cheaper
2 slower
3 larger/bigger
4 better
5 earlier
6 more difficult/harder

D 1 The journey to Leeds is long, much longer than I thought.
2 You have the same jacket as me.
3 This year we are staying in a hotel further away from the beach than last year.
4 My sister and I are twins, but she is much thinner than me.
5 Last year we had the worst harvest since 1990.

Exercises 41

A 1 a
2 a
3 a
4 b
5 a
6 a

B 1 I'm often busy.
2 I probably won't be able to come tomorrow.
3 He speaks Spanish very well.
4 Jane and I meet every week.
5 I didn't go to work yesterday.
6 We've just bought a small sailing boat.

C 1 A: [ ] [√]
B: [√] [ ]
2 A: [√] [ ]
B: [ ] [√]
3 A: [√] [ ]
B: [√] [ ]
4 A: [ ] [√]
B: [ ] [√]
5 A: [ ] [√]
B: [ ] [√]

D 1 I've already read (AE: I already read) this book.
2 I often go on holiday (AE: on vacation)in winter.
3 Mary goes to Manchester every week.
4 I saw Tom at the cinema (AE: at the movies / at the movie theater) yesterday.
5 Perhaps we will visit our friends in America next year.

Exercises 42

A 1 a
2 a
3 a
4 b
5 b
6 a

B 1 homework✗, progress✗✗
2 advice✗, information✗
3 works✗
4 progress✗✗, help✗, people✗, proof✗

C 1 A: looks
B: it
2 A: homework
B: information
3 A: another piece of bread
B: such lovely weather
4 A: such good Italian
B: spaghetti

D
1 Do they have / Have they got enough proof that he's the murderer?
2 You have made (AE: you made) a lot of progress this year.
3 She always buys expensive material.
4 My hair is much too long.
5 He speaks French well and his knowledge of Spanish isn't bad.

Exercises 43

A
1 b
2 a
3 b
4 b
5 a
6 b

B
1 are
2 is
3 is
4 is
5 have
6 are
8 is
9 look

C
1 are
2 were
3 are
4 is
5 are
6 Are

D
1 More than three million people are unemployed here.
2 The United States has never had (AE: never had) a female president.
3 The right clothes are very important for an interview.
4 Are these your binoculars?
5 The police in England aren't armed.

Exercises 44

A
1 b
2 a
3 a
4 a
5 a
6 a

B
1 some, any, anywhere
2 something, anything
3 some, some, any, some
4 anyone, anyone
5 anything, something

C
1 A: something
B: any
2 A: anyone
B: someone
3 A: anywhere
B: somewhere, something
4 A: some
B: someone
5 A: anything
B: any

D
1 Is there a (tele)phone box (AE: (tele)phone booth / pay phone) anywhere?
2 We have hardly any furniture in our new flat (AE: apartment).
3 I haven't learned/learnt (AE: I didn't learn) any grammar this week.
4 If there's still some cheese in the fridge, you don't have/need to / needn't (AE: don't have/need to) buy any.
5 I haven't heard anything from Susan for two months. Have you heard anything?

Exercises 45

A
1 a
2 b
3 a
4 b
5 b
6 a

B
1 most
2 None
3 every ten minutes
4 enough work
5 most of the questions
6 a lot of people

C
1 many police
2 a lot
3 every match
4 enough time, most things
5 None of, a lot of

D
1 Most people / Most of the people here are from Spain.
2 None of us understood the homework.
3 I go to the hairdresser's every two months.
4 You can leave your bag here. I've got / I have enough room.
5 She knows a lot about politics.

Exercises 46

A
1 a
2 a
3 a
4 b
5 a
6 a

B
2 all ~~the~~ German children
3 ~~the~~ both cars
6 ~~the~~ both girls

C
1 Both my brothers / My brothers both live abroad.
2 We all work really hard in our office.
3 We all left the building when the fire alarm rang.
4 My sister and I both moved last year.
5 We've all passed the exam.
6 My mother and father both / Both my mother and father have problems with their health.

D
1 I would do anything to meet him.
2 Both (of) my neighbours (AE: neighbors) are / My neighbours (AE: neighbors) are both very friendly.
3 All (of) my friends / My friends all wanted to help. Everybody came.
4 We both / Both of us bought a new car last year.
5 Which suitcase do you want? You can have either – the red one or the black one.

Exercises 47

A
1 b
2 b
3 a
4 b
5 a
6 b

B
1 ~~the~~ work, ~~the~~ bed
3 in ~~the~~ hospital (AE: in the hospital)
4 ~~the~~ Oxford University
5 ~~the~~ Downing Street
6 ~~The~~ music, ~~the~~ classical music

C
1 Turkey, breakfast, dinner
2 university, the United States, the Rocky Mountains
3 people, Trafalgar Square
4 by car, the train, lunch
5 Life, hospital (AE: the hospital)

D
1 Is Mont Blanc in Switzerland?
2 British cuisine is better than people think.
3 I love music. I play the guitar (AE: I play guitar) every day.
4 I never take the bus – I always go to work by car.
5 My neighbour is in prison. Life is hard there.

Exercises 48

A
1 b
2 b
3 a
4 a
5 b
6 b

B
1 A: such a lovely day
B: such a long way, half an hour
2 A: a member
B: once a week
3 A: As a student, a drinker
B: an alcoholic, an anarchist
4 A: half a
B: a kilo
5 A: an expert
B: an optimist, such good weather

C
1 I got such a shock when I heard about Sue's divorce. As a sales manager, she's away from home at least twice a month – perhaps that's the reason.
2 Tom is such an idiot. He had an accident yesterday – he was driving over 120 kilometres an hour!
3 As a child, I had to help at home. My parents had a shop and worked six days a week.
4 Mary is an atheist and her husband is a strict Muslim.
5 We got a real surprise yesterday. Our daughter, who is a student in America, came home for my birthday. It's half a year since we last saw her.
6 I've got a terrible headache. I think I'm getting a cold. It's not surprising – we've had such awful weather recently.

D
1 I have / have got a headache. – You work too much: 50 hours a week.
2 We had such great weather yesterday. The day was so nice! / It was such a nice day!
3 As a pensioner (AE: retiree) my mother is never at home (AE: never home)!
4 I have such a good doctor. Her husband is a doctor too.
5 My cousin (has) married an Englishman. He speaks good German.

Grammatik flexibel lernen, üben, wiederholen

Grammar – no problem ist eine Übungsgrammatik, mit der die wichtigsten Strukturen der englischen Grundgrammatik gelernt, geübt und gefestigt werden können. Das Buch ist flexibel einsetzbar:

- zur Einführung und Einübung neuer Grammmatik; und/oder zur Wiederholung und Vertiefung bereits gelernter Grammatik
- kursbuchbegleitend; und/oder als selbstständiges Lernmittel
- im Unterricht; und/oder im Selbststudium.

Grammar – no problem ist speziell auf die Bedürfnisse deutschsprachiger Lernender ausgerichtet und geht auf typische Fehler ein, wie sie immer wieder bei deutschen Muttersprachlern auftauchen.

Inhalt und Aufbau

Grammar – no problem enthält 48 Lektionen, die alle wichtigen Bereiche der Grundgrammatik abdecken. Jede Unit ist als übersichtliche Doppelseite angelegt – auf der linken Seite finden Sie Erklärungen (auf Deutsch) mit Beispielsätzen und auf der rechten Seite Übungen. Jede linke Seite wird mit einem Dialog eröffnet, der typische Fehler bewusst macht und korrigiert. Danach folgen ausführliche Erläuterungen auf Deutsch zum Gebrauch der Struktur mit vielen Beispielsätzen. Das Symbol ! und die Farbe Rot weisen dabei auf besondere Fehlerquellen hin. Am Fuß der Seite werden die Hauptpunkte unter **Das Wichtigste in Kürze** noch einmal zusammengefasst.

Auf der rechten Seite finden Sie abwechslungsreiche Übungen mit ansteigendem Schwierigkeitsgrad: Fehleranalyse, praktische Anwendung, Übersetzung. Die Übungssätze sind Beispiele natürlicher Kommunikationssituationen. Die Lösungen können meist direkt ins Buch geschrieben werden; der beigelegte Schlüssel (mit Alternativlösungen im amerikanischen Englisch) hilft Ihnen, Ihre Antworten zu kontrollieren.

Auf der Seite 103 finden Sie Hinweise zu den Grammatikbereichen, bei denen es Unterschiede zwischen britischem und amerikanischem Englisch gibt. Auf den Seiten 104 – 109 steht der ausführliche Index in Deutsch und Englisch. Auf Seite 110 finden Sie eine Übersicht über die verwendeten grammatikalischen Begriffe und auf Seite 111 eine Übersicht über Schreibbesonderheiten des Englischen. Die wichtigsten unregelmäßigen Verben können Sie sich als Lesezeichen herausschneiden.

Die Arbeit mit dem Buch

Wenn Sie das Buch in einem Kurs oder im Einzelunterricht verwenden, wird Ihnen Ihr(e) Kursleiter(in) sagen, wie Sie damit arbeiten, aber auch im Selbststudium können Sie **Grammar – no problem** effektiv einsetzen. Sie müssen das Buch nicht der Reihe nach durcharbeiten, sondern können Schwerpunkte setzen. In den einzelnen Lektionen finden Sie immer Hinweise auf andere Kapitel, in denen ähnliche oder weiterführende Themen behandelt werden.

- Schauen Sie sich das Inhaltsverzeichnis an und suchen Sie sich ein Thema (eine Lektion) aus, das (die) Sie bearbeiten wollen.
- Lesen Sie die Dialoge in Ruhe durch und denken Sie über die Fehler nach.
- Arbeiten Sie die deutschen Erklärungen durch. Ausführliche Beispielsätze helfen die grammatischen Strukturen zu verstehen und anzuwenden. Machen Sie die Übungen auf der rechten Seite.
- Mit Hilfe des Lösungsschlüssels können Sie sich selbst kontrollieren.
- Wenn Sie Fehler gemacht haben, lesen Sie die Erklärungen noch einmal durch.
- Wenn Sie glauben, dass Sie ein grammatisches Kapitel schon beherrschen, können Sie auch zuerst die Übungen machen und mit dem Schlüssel vergleichen. Vergessen Sie trotzdem nicht, die Erklärungen zu lesen, denn Sie helfen Ihnen, Ihr Wissen zu strukturieren.

INHALT

1 Simple present
Einfache Gegenwart

A: Where's Jim this morning?
B: He ~~work~~ [works] on Saturdays.
A: Oh.
B: Well, in the morning. He ~~works not~~ [doesn't work] in the afternoon.
A: Can I phone him?
B: Yes. ~~Know you~~ [Do you know] his phone number?

Form

■ he/she/it mit -s	Ann loves music. She plays the piano. *Ann liebt Musik. Sie spielt Klavier.*
■ Verneinung mit don't und doesn't	I don't work on Mondays. *Montags arbeite ich nicht.* Tom doesn't drink coffee, only tea. *Tom trinkt keinen Kaffee, nur Tee.*
■ Fragen mit do und does	Do tourists spend much here? *Geben Touristen hier viel Geld aus?* When does school start? At nine? *Wann beginnt die Schule? Um neun?*
■ Kurzantworten mit do und does (+ not)	Do they know? – Yes, they do. / No, they don't. *Wissen sie es? – Ja./Nein.* Does Ed eat meat? – Yes, he does. / No, he doesn't. *Isst Ed Fleisch? – Ja./Nein.*

Gebrauch

■ **Mit der einfachen Gegenwart beschreibt man einen Dauerzustand.**

Feststehende Tatsachen	The sun goes down in the west. *Die Sonne geht im Westen unter.*
Gewohnheiten	I usually leave the house at 7.15. *Ich verlasse das Haus meist um 7.15 Uhr.*
Regelmäßige Vorgänge	On Mondays banks open later. *Montags machen die Banken später auf.*
Bräuche	In Spain people have supper later. *In Spanien isst man später zu Abend.*
Berufsangaben	My cousin works for Microsoft. *Meine Kusine arbeitet bei Microsoft.*
Angaben zu Hobbys	My wife sings in a choir. *Meine Frau singt in einem Chor.*

Signalwörter

■ Ausdrücke der Häufigkeit	always, usually, normally, mostly, often, sometimes, rarely, never, hardly ever, every day, every morning, every time
■ Uhr- und Tageszeiten	at six o'clock, in the morning, at breakfast time, before school, after work
■ Wochentage, Monate, Jahreszeiten, Feste	on Monday(s), on weekdays, at the weekend, in June, in the summer, at Easter, before Christmas

■ **Stellung: Ausdrücke der Häufigkeit (außer solchen mit every) stehen meist vor dem letzten Verbteil. Alle anderen (einschl. Ausdrücke mit every) stehen meist am Satzende.**

I don't often see Alan at work. I see Ann every day / at lunch / on Monday.

! Ein Signalwort kann nicht zwischen Verb und Objekt stehen!

~~I buy always two newspapers.~~ I always buy two newspapers.
~~I read every day two newspapers.~~ I read two newspapers every day.

Das Wichtigste in Kürze

- he/she/it mit -s; Fragen/Verneinung mit einer Form von do
- Häufigkeitsausdrücke (außer every ...) vor dem Verb; kein Signalwort zwischen Verb und Objekt!

Weitere Informationen → Units 3-4

A One sentence has a mistake. Which sentence is correct?

a I doesn't like ice cream.
b I don't like ice cream. ✓

1 a He lives in Berlin.
b He live in Berlin.

2 a We don't like football.
b We not like football.

3 a Where live you?
b Where do you live?

4 a What means 'bicycle'?
b What does 'bicycle' mean?

5 a I always start work at 8 o'clock.
b I start always work at 8 o'clock.

6 a She doesn't usually work at weekends.
b She doesn't work usually at weekends.

B Make negative sentences.

I come from Austria.
I don't come from Austria.

1 I normally go to bed before 10 o'clock.
2 This book teaches vocabulary.
3 I go to work by train.
4 We usually have an English lesson on Tuesday.
5 My sisters live in Manchester.

Now ask questions.

Where / you / come from?
Where do you come from?

6 What time / you / go to bed?
7 What / this book / teach?
8 How / you / go to work?
9 When / you / usually have an English lesson?
10 Where / your sisters / live?

C Complete these dialogues with the verbs in the correct form.

A: I don't understand this letter. Can you help me?
B: I'm sorry. I *don't speak* (not speak) Spanish.

1 A: Where does your sister live?
B: She .... (live) in America.

2 A: Excuse me. Where is the post office?
B: I'm sorry. I .... (not know).

3 A: Can we meet on Saturday morning?
B: No, I'm afraid not. I ....
(always work) on Saturdays.

4 A: What time is it, please?
B: I'm sorry. I .... (not have) a watch.

5 A: Would you like a cigarette?
B: No, thanks. I .... (not smoke).

6 A: Good morning. Can I speak to David, please?
B: No, I'm afraid he .... (not work) here any more.

D Give short answers.

Do you live in Berlin? – No, *I don't.*

1 Does Ann still work for IBM? – No, ...
2 Do you have much snow here? – Yes, ...
3 Do your children like school? – No, ...
4 Does your boss travel a lot? – Yes, ...
5 Do you enjoy your work? Yes, ...
6 Does your wife speak French? No, ...

E Write questions for these answers.

A: Where *do you live*? B: We live in Dresden.

1 A: When .... work?
B: I usually start work at 8.30.

2 A: How .... to work?
B: Paul? He goes to work by train.

3 A: How many children ....?
B: They have two children.

4 A: How often .... tennis?
B: We play tennis once a week.

5 A: What .... at weekends?
B: At weekends? I often work in the garden.

2 Present continuous
Verlaufsform der Gegenwart

A: Are we all here? Where's Pete?

B: He ~~is coming not~~ *isn't coming* this week.

A: Oh. Why?

B: He ~~works~~ *is working* in Paris this week.

A: Oh, OK. Let's start the meeting then.

B: What ~~discuss we~~ *are we discussing* today?

Form

■ Form von be + Verb mit Endung -ing*	Listen. Stan is singing in the bath. *Horch. Stan singt in der Badewanne.* Leave me alone. I'm working. *Lass mich in Ruhe. Ich arbeite (gerade).*
■ Verneinung: Form von be + not	You aren't (= are not) listening. *Du hörst nicht zu.* The bus isn't (= is not) stopping. Hey! *Der Bus hält nicht. He!*
■ Fragebildung durch Umstellung	Ed is watching TV. *Ed sieht (gerade) fern.* Is Ed watching TV? – Yes, he is. / No, he isn't. *Sieht Ed (gerade) fern? – Ja./Nein.*

*Schreibbesonderheiten: siehe Seite 111

Gebrauch

■ Mit der Verlaufsform der Gegenwart beschreibt man ein momentanes Geschehen, das jetzt im Verlauf begriffen und noch nicht abgeschlossen ist, oder eine vorübergehende Situation.

Momentanes Geschehen	What are you doing? – I'm repairing this chair. *Was machst du (gerade)? – Ich repariere (gerade) diesen Stuhl.* Look! It's snowing. *Schau! Es schneit.*
Vorübergehende Situation	I'm on a diet, so I'm eating a lot of salad at the moment. *Ich mache eine Diät, also esse ich zur Zeit viel Salat.* Ann's working in Berlin this week. *Ann arbeitet diese Woche in Berlin.* Tom is learning Chinese. *Tom lernt Chinesisch.*

Signalwörter

■ Angaben für jetzt	now, at the moment, just
■ Angaben für nicht abgeschlossene Zeiträume	today, this week, this month, this year, this summer

■ Stellung: just steht vor dem letzten Verbteil, alle anderen Signalwörter am Satzanfang oder -ende.

I am just making the tea. — I'm not working at the moment / today.

! Ein Signalwort kann nicht zwischen Verb und Objekt stehen!

~~I am finishing just my supper.~~	I am just finishing my supper.
~~We are eating today fish.~~	We are eating fish today.

Das Wichtigste in Kürze

■ Form von be + Verb mit Endung -ing

■ Die Handlung/Situation ist jetzt gerade im Verlauf begriffen / nicht abgeschlossen / vorübergehend

Weitere Informationen → Units 3-4

A One sentence has a mistake. Which sentence is correct?

a What you are reading?
b What are you reading? ✔

1 **a** My son isn't studying in Germany.
b My son is studying not in Germany.

2 **a** We are today talking about the new project.
b We are talking about the new project today.

3 **a** I'm just finishing the report.
b I'm finishing just the report.

4 **a** Take your umbrella. It raining.
b Take your umbrella. It's raining.

5 **a** Where you are going?
b Where are you going?

6 **a** This week are the children staying at home.
b This week the children are staying at home.

B Make negative sentences.

I'm learning French.
I'm not learning French.

1 I'm working in Leipzig this week.
2 The children are watching Sesame Street.
3 The Pope is visiting Thailand at the moment.
4 We are working from 8 till 3 this week.
5 I'm learning English for fun.

Now ask questions.

What / you / learn?
What are you learning?

6 Where / you / work this week?
7 What / the children / watch?
8 Which country / the Pope / visit?
9 When / you / work this week?
10 Why / you / learn English?

C Complete these dialogues with the verbs in the correct form.

A: You can't go out! You're ill.
B: It's all right. I*'m going* (go) to the doctor's.

1 A: What's your brother doing now?
B: He .... (study) in America.

2 A: Hurry up or we'll miss the bus!
B: I'm sorry. I .... (look for) my keys.

3 A: Can we play tennis on Saturday morning?
B: No, I'm afraid not. I .... (work) on Saturdays this month.

4 A: .... (you/wait) for the bus?
B: No. I .... (wait) for a friend but she is late.

D Give short answers.

Are you enjoying the party? –
No, *I'm not.*

1 Is Carol working this weekend? –
Yes, ...

2 Are you still learning French? –
Yes, ...

3 Is it still snowing? –
No, ...

4 Are you both going home now? –
Yes, ...

E Write questions for these answers.

A: What *is Pete studying*?
B: Pete is studying Economics.

1 A: Why .... French?
B: Joe? He's learning it for fun.

2 A: Where .... this week?
B: Jane? She's working in Hull.

3 A: Who .... for?
B: I'm waiting for Thomas.

4 A: What time .... ?
B: We're meeting at 10 o'clock.

3 Simple present – Present continuous (1)
Einfache Gegenwart – Verlaufsform der Gegenwart (1)

A: OK, can you all sit down, please? The pizza is ready.
B: Mm. You ~~are always making~~ always make lovely pizzas, Jill.
A: Thanks, Ann. Red wine or white wine with it?
B: Usually I ~~am drinking~~ drink white, but today I'd like red.
A: OK. And you, Tom?
B: Water for him! He ~~drives~~ is driving tonight!

Einfache Gegenwart: Dauerzustand

- Mit der einfachen Gegenwart beschreibt man
  1. regelmäßige und sich wiederholende Vorgänge, die zusammen eine bestimmte Situation bilden
  2. Dauerzustände.

Feststehende Tatsachen:
I **come** from Germany.

Gewohnheiten:
I **don't eat** much chocolate.

Regelmäßige Vorgänge:
The cinema **shows** a lot of foreign films.

Bräuche:
People **don't celebrate** Christmas in Japan.

Berufsangaben:
She's a writer. She **writes** detective stories.

Angaben zu Hobbys und Freizeitaktivitäten:
Don **plays** a lot of tennis.

Verlaufsform: Momentanes Geschehen

- Mit der Verlaufsform beschreibt man
  1. einen augenblicklichen Einzelvorgang, der im Verlauf begriffen und nicht abgeschlossen ist
  2. eine vorübergehende Situation.

Augenblickliche Vorgänge:
Hello, Ann. I**'m phoning** from London.
What **are** you **doing** on the floor?
He **isn't reading**. Look, his eyes are shut.
We**'re waiting** for Don. He has the key.

Vorübergehende Situationen:
Shall I meet you at your hotel? – No. I**'m not staying** at a hotel this time. I**'m staying** with friends.
The weather is so nice that I**'m cycling** to work this week.
Phil **is playing** a lot of tennis at the moment because he**'s trying** to get fit again.

Einfache Form und Verlaufsform im Vergleich

Ann **works** for Siemens in Munich.	→	She **is working** on a new project now.
I **don't** usually **enjoy** parties.	→	But I**'m enjoying** this one.
It **doesn't snow** here much.	→	But it**'s snowing** now.
At Tim's school they **learn** two foreign languages.	→	Tim **is learning** French and Spanish.
I usually **get up** at six.	→	This week I**'m getting up** late. I'm on holiday.

! Eine feste berufliche Situation wird immer mit der einfachen Gegenwart ausgedrückt; eine vorübergehende oder nicht abgeschlossene Lern- oder Ausbildungssituation mit der Verlaufsform.

Don **works** for VW. He **designs** cars.	→	Don's daughter is a student. She **is studying** design. She **is training** to be a designer.

Das Wichtigste in Kürze

- Einfache Gegenwart: etwas geschieht in bestimmten Abständen = Dauersituation/Dauerzustand
- Verlaufsform: etwas ist jetzt gerade im Verlauf begriffen, nicht abgeschlossen, vorübergehend

Weitere Informationen → Unit 4

A One sentence has a mistake. Which sentence is correct?

a I'm coming from England – I was born in Bristol.
b I come from England – I was born in Bristol. ✔

1 **a** I live in Bonn. Where do you live?
b I live in Bonn. Where are you living?

2 **a** We are saving to buy a new car.
b We save to buy a new car.

3 **a** My sister learns English for her job.
b My sister is learning English for her job.

4 **a** I often watch English films.
b I'm often watching English films.

5 **a** Their children never help at home.
b Their children are never helping at home.

6 **a** My boss is travelling a lot at the moment.
b My boss travels a lot at the moment.

B What usually happens and what is happening today, this week ...?

(usually) I / finish work at 5 o'clock
(this week) I / finish at 4 o'clock
I usually finish work at 5 o'clock. This week I'm finishing at 4 o'clock.

1 (usually) we / go shopping on Fridays
(this week) we / go on Saturday
2 (always) John / go to work by car
(today) he / go by bus because his car is at the garage
3 (sometimes) the children / visit their grandparents
(this Sunday) they / stay at home
4 (this year) Jane / go to Australia for Christmas
(often) she / spend Christmas abroad
5 (this week) I / not work on Friday
(never) I / work on Mondays, so that means I can have a long weekend

C Complete these dialogues. Put the verbs in the simple present or the present continuous.

1 A: Would you like to come to the cinema this evening?
B: I'm sorry, I can't. My sister .... (stay) with us at the moment.
A: How long .... (she/stay)?

2 A: Hello, Petra! Where .... (you/go)?
B: I .... (go) to my evening class. I .... (learn) Italian.
A: Really? I .... (go) to an Italian class once a week too.

3 A: .... (you/normally/go) on holiday in the summer?
B: Yes, we .... (usually spend) a month in France, but this year we .... (stay) here.
A: Yes, this year we .... (not go) on holiday, either.

4 A: Where .... (your brother/work)?
B: He .... (work) for a big computer company. And your sister?
A: She .... (not work) at the moment. She's unemployed.

D Translate the following sentences.

1 Dieses Jahr fahren wir nicht in Urlaub, weil wir umziehen.
2 Heute schneit es viel. Normalerweise schneit es nicht so viel im März.
3 Mein Bruder spricht drei Sprachen. Jetzt lernt er eine vierte – Russisch.
4 Was machst du dieses Wochenende? Bleibst du zuhause?
5 Heute Abend gehen wir in ein vegetarisches Restaurant, weil unsere Freunde kein Fleisch essen.

4 Simple present – Present continuous (2)
Einfache Gegenwart – Verlaufsform der Gegenwart (2)

A: Can we meet tonight?
B: Sorry I ~~am having~~ have no time today.
A: Tomorrow then? We could have a drink at the pub.
B: It ~~is depending~~ depends on the time. After nine is OK.
A: OK. 9.30 at the Crown? No, you don't like the Crown, do you?
B: Oh, now I~~'m thinking~~ think it's quite nice, with the new owner.

Verben, die nicht in der Verlaufsform gebraucht werden

- Verben, die keine Tätigkeit bezeichnen, werden nicht in der Verlaufsform gebraucht.

– Verben des Brauchens, Wollens und Mögens	I **need** a drink. I **want** some beer. I **like** beer.
– Verben des Meinens, Wissens, Glaubens	I **think** Ed is right, but I **don't know**. I **believe** him.
– Verben der Sinneswahrnehmung	**Does** that **taste** good? It **smells** funny.
– Verben, die Eigenschaften und Zustände ausdrücken	This **looks** like Italian. What **does** it **mean**?

need *brauchen*	**think** *glauben, meinen*	**see** *sehen*	**be** *sein*
want *wollen*	**know** *wissen, kennen*	**hear** *hören*	**have** *haben*
wish *wünschen*	**remember** *sich erinnern*	**feel** *fühlen, sich anfühlen*	**seem** *erscheinen*
like *mögen*	**understand** *verstehen*	**smell** *riechen*	**consist of** *bestehen aus*
love *lieben*	**believe** *glauben, meinen*	**taste** *schmecken*	**mean** *bedeuten*
hate *hassen*	**realize** *erkennen, begreifen*		**belong to** *gehören*
prefer *vorziehen*	**see** *verstehen*		**depend on** *abhängen von*

! Einige dieser Verben haben mehr als eine Bedeutung, d.h. sie bezeichnen in einer Bedeutung einen Zustand (keine Verlaufsform möglich), in einer anderen eine Tätigkeit (Verlaufsform möglich).

	Zustand: Keine Verlaufsform	**Tätigkeit: Verlaufsform**
have	I **have** no time now. *(haben)*	I **am having** a bath/shower. *(nehmen)*
	Ann **has** a big family. *(haben)*	They **are having** lunch / a cup of tea. *(essen/trinken)*
	We **have** a big double room. *(haben)*	We **are having a nice time**. *(sich amüsieren)*
	They **have** lots of money. *(haben)*	They **are having a party** again. *(eine Party feiern)*
	Tom **has** an awful boss. *(haben)*	They **are having an argument** again. *(sich streiten)*
think	What **does** Don **think**? *(meinen)*	Quiet! He **is thinking**. *(nachdenken)*
	We **think** the flat is small. *(meinen)*	We **are thinking of** moving. *(sich überlegen)*
see	Now I **see** where the hole is. Here. *(sehen = wahrnehmen)*	I **am** not **seeing** much of Jim at the moment. *(sehen = treffen)*
	I **see** what you're trying to say. *(sehen = verstehen)*	We**'re seeing** more online shopping than ever before. *(sehen = erleben)*
look	This building **looks** old. *(aussehen)*	Ann **is looking** out of the window. *(schauen)*

Das Wichtigste in Kürze

- Keine Verlaufsform bei Verben, die keine Tätigkeit, sondern einen Zustand ausdrücken
- Bei Verben mit mehreren Bedeutungen: Tätigkeit = Verlaufsform – Zustand = keine Verlaufsform

A One sentence has a mistake. Which sentence is correct?

a This book looks interesting. – Yes, it's really good. ✔
b This book is looking interesting. – Yes, it's really good.

1 **a** This wine tastes very strange.
b This wine is tasting very strange.

2 **a** What's the matter? What do you think about?
b What's the matter? What are you thinking about?

3 **a** I'm seeing Lynn this evening. It's her birthday.
b I see Lynn this evening. It's her birthday.

4 **a** You don't seem very happy. Are you OK?
b You aren't seeming very happy. Are you OK?

5 **a** My daughter doesn't want to go to the wedding.
b My daughter isn't wanting to go to the wedding.

6 **a** I'm sorry, she doesn't have time at the moment.
b I'm sorry, she isn't having time at the moment.

B Complete these sentences with the correct form of the verb.

think I'm thinking about our next holiday – it'll be great!
I think we should book our flights soon.

1 look What a fantastic garden you have! It .... wonderful.
My wife loves roses – she .... at your rose garden at the moment.

2 see Now I .... what the problem is – I'll talk to Joe again.
I .... him this week – we're on a course together.

3 think I'm worried about work. I .... our firm may close.
I .... of looking for a new job.

4 have Listen, Sue and Jack .... another argument.
They .... so many problems.

C Complete these dialogues. Put the verbs in the simple present or the present continuous.

1 A: What .... (you/think)? Should we buy the red sofa or the blue one?
B: I .... (prefer) the red one but it is too expensive.

2 A: What .... (this word/mean)? I .... (not understand) this sentence.
B: I .... (not know) but I .... (think) it's a kind of fruit.

3 A: Your sister .... (not seem) very happy at the moment. Is she OK?
B: Yes, she's just tired. I .... (see) her this evening to talk about a holiday. We .... (think) about a camping holiday in France.

4 A: .... (you/remember) what time we are meeting Carol and Steve?
B: I'm not sure. I .... (have) lunch with Carol today. I'll ask her.

5 A: I'm going shopping. .... (you/need) anything?
B: I .... (just think). No, I .... (not think) so, thanks.

D Translate the following sentences.

1 Dieses Buch gehört mir nicht. Gehört es dir?
2 Ich denke über Anns Frage nach. Ich denke, wir brauchen mehr Zeit.
3 Hast du heute Abend Zeit? – Es hängt von meiner Arbeit ab.
4 Warum schaust du dieses Auto an? – Weil es so toll aussieht. Aber ich meine, es ist zu teuer.
5 Frühstückt Tom noch (*still*)? – Nein, ich glaube er ist fertig. Das bedeutet, wir können gehen.

5 Simple past
Einfache Vergangenheit

A: Did you ~~went~~ go to Angela's party ~~for two days~~ two days ago?
B: Yes, it was great. But you weren't there.

A: I didn't ~~had~~ have time. Too much work.
B: That's a pity.

A: Jill said some people ~~felt~~ fell in the swimming pool. ~~Did you be~~ Were you one of them?
B: Me? Why do you think that?

Form

Verb **be**: **was/were**	I **was** surprised; the others **were** older. *Ich war überrascht; die anderen waren älter.*
Regelmäßige Verben: Grundform + **-ed***	We **worked** hard yesterday. *Wir haben gestern hart gearbeitet.* The rain **stopped** at six. *Der Regen hörte um sechs auf.*
Unregelmäßige Verben: besondere Formen (s.u.)	Tom **rang** earlier. *Tom hat vorhin angerufen.* I **forgot** to tell you. *Ich habe vergessen, es dir zu sagen.*
Verneinung: **was/were** + **not** sonst **didn't** + Infinitiv	I **wasn't** here yesterday. *Ich war gestern nicht hier.* The neighbours **weren't** at home. *Die Nachbarn waren nicht zuhause.* Bernd **didn't come** last week. *Bernd ist letzte Woche nicht gekommen.*
Fragen, Kurzantworten: Verb **be**: **was/were** sonst **did** (+ Infinitiv)	Where **was** Andy? *Wo war Andy?* **Were** you here? – Yes, I **was**. / No, I **wasn't**. *Warst du hier? – Ja./Nein.* **Did** Ed **phone**? – Yes, he **did**. / No, he **didn't**. *Hat Ed angerufen? – Ja./Nein.*

* Schreibbesonderheiten: siehe Seite 111

Unregelmäßige Verben (vollständige Liste siehe Umschlagklappe/Lesezeichen)

be	**was/were**	fall	**fell**	go	**went**	make	**made**	stand	**stood**
buy	**bought**	feel	**felt**	grow	**grew**	meet	**met**	take	**took**
come	**came**	forget	**forgot**	have	**had**	ring	**rang**	tell	**told**
cost	**cost**	get	**got**	know	**knew**	say	**said**	think	**thought**
do	**did**	give	**gave**	leave	**left**	see	**saw**	write	**wrote**

Gebrauch und Signalwörter

- Mit der einfachen Vergangenheit beschreibt man abgeschlossene Ereignisse und Zustände.
- Typische Signalwörter bezeichnen einen Zeitpunkt oder Zeitraum der abgeschlossenen Vergangenheit.

yesterday und **last ...**	yesterday, last week, last month, last year, last night, last Tuesday, last weekend
Ausdrücke mit **ago**	two hours ago, a few weeks ago, several months ago, ten years ago
when?, Daten	when?, (at) what time?, in 1998, on 28 December, in April

! Signalwörter stehen am Satzende oder -anfang, nicht zwischen Verb und Objekt.
I saw Jill **last week**. (~~I saw last week Jill.~~)

! **ago** steht immer am Ende der Zeitbestimmung: We met two days **ago** (~~for two days~~). ... *vor zwei Tagen.*

Das Wichtigste in Kürze

- Regelmäßige Verben: **-ed**; unregelmäßige Verben: besondere Formen; Fragen/Verneinung mit **did**
- Gebrauch, wenn etwas zu einem bestimmten Zeitpunkt der Vergangenheit abgeschlossen wurde

Weitere Informationen → Units 8, 10

A One sentence has a mistake. Which sentence is correct?

a I didn't went to school yesterday.
b I didn't go to school yesterday. ✔

1 **a** He bought his car for two years.
b He bought his car two years ago.

2 **a** We weren't at home last night.
b We didn't be at home last night.

3 **a** We stood in a lovely hotel last year.
b We stayed in a lovely hotel last year.

4 **a** What did you last weekend?
b What did you do last weekend?

5 **a** Julie fell downstairs last week.
b Julie felt downstairs last week.

6 **a** Where was you born?
b Where were you born?

B Make negative sentences.

I was at home yesterday.
I wasn't at home yesterday.

1 I got up early yesterday.
2 This jacket was expensive.
3 Sam went to the USA last year.
4 Judy rang Clive last week.

Now ask questions.

Where / you / be yesterday?
Where were you yesterday?

5 What time / you / get up yesterday?
6 How much / be / your jacket?
7 Where / Sam / go last year?
8 Who / Judy / ring last week?

C Complete these dialogues with the verbs in the correct form.

A: What *did you do* (you/do) last Sunday?
B: I *visited* (visit) some old friends.

1 A: What .... (your son/give) you for your birthday?
B: Nothing! He .... (forget).

2 A: That's a nice pullover. Where .... (you/buy) it?
B: I .... (not buy) it. It .... (be) a present.

3 A: I .... (try) to call you yesterday but you .... (not be) at work.
B: No, I .... (stay) at home because I .... (feel) ill.

4 A: .... (you/have) a good weekend?
B: Lovely, thanks. We .... (have) visitors on Saturday and on Sunday we .... (not do) anything.

5 A: What time .... (you/get) home last night?
B: Late. We .... (leave) at midnight and .... (miss) the last bus.

D Write questions for these answers.

A: Where *did you grow up*? B: I grew up in Perth.

1 A: When .... this course?
B: This course? I started five years ago.

2 A: How much .... ?
B: My coat? It cost £350.

3 A: .... Tom at the party?
B: No, I didn't see him.

4 A: .... by cheque?
B: No, I paid by credit card.

E Give short answers.

Did you phone Sue? – No, *I didn't.*

1 Was Ann away last week? – No, ...
2 Did the taxi come on time? – Yes, ...
3 Were you born here? – No, ...
4 Did you go to the bank? – Yes, ...
5 Did Ed give you my message? – Yes, ...
6 Did you both work late? – No, ...

6 Past continuous
Verlaufsform der Vergangenheit

A: Did you have a good evening with Julie and Dave?

B: Not really. I left work late. And when I was driving to the restaurant, I ~~was having~~ had an accident.

A: Oh no! What happened?

B: A man in another car drove into me when I ~~waited~~ was waiting at some traffic lights.

A: Didn't he see you?

B: No, he ~~spoke~~ was speaking to someone on his mobile phone and ~~didn't concentrate~~ wasn't concentrating on the road.

Form

■ **was/were ...ing**	When Sandra came home, I **was cooking** and the children **were helping** me.
■ Verneinung	I **wasn't watching** TV. They **weren't playing**.
■ Fragen, Kurzantworten	**Were** you **cooking**? – Yes, I **was**. **Were** the children **playing**? – No, they **weren't**.

Gebrauch

■ **Mit der Verlaufsform der Vergangenheit beschreibt man Handlungen und Vorgänge, die zu einem Zeitpunkt der Vergangenheit im Verlauf begriffen, nicht abgeschlossen waren, (vorübergehend) andauerten.**

– Im Verlauf begriffene, nicht abgeschlossene Handlungen/Vorgänge	It **was raining** when I left the office. *Es regnete (gerade), als ich das Büro verließ.* We **were** still **playing** poker at 3 am. *Nachts um 3 spielten wir immer noch Poker.* Tom **was smoking** when I saw him. *Tom rauchte (gerade), als ich ihn sah.*
– Vorübergehende Situationen	We **were living** with friends because our new flat wasn't ready. *Wir wohnten (gerade/vorübergehend) bei Freunden, weil unsere neue Wohnung nicht fertig war.*
– Andauernde Handlungen	What **were** you **doing** in Tim's room all that time? – I **was reading** to him. *Was hast du die ganze Zeit in Tims Zimmer gemacht? – Ich habe ihm vorgelesen.*

Verlaufsform und einfache Form im Vergleich

■ **Oft benutzt man die Verlaufsform, wenn eine Situation von etwas unterbrochen wurde. Die bereits verlaufende „Hintergrund-Situation" steht in der Verlaufsform, das neue Geschehen in der einfachen Form.**

We **were having** supper when the phone **rang**.
I **was standing** at the traffic lights when the accident **happened**.
While we **were waiting**, it **started** to rain.

■ **Zwei nacheinander eintretende Geschehen werden beide mit der einfachen Form ausgedrückt.**
A car **stopped** and a man **got out**.

Vgl. When I went in, everybody **was standing** at the window. They **were looking** at something outside.
When I went in, everybody **stood up**. They all **looked** at me as if I came from Mars.

! **Die Verlaufsform ist bei Zustandsverben normalerweise nicht möglich (siehe Unit 4).**
When I last saw Tom he **seemed** (~~was seeming~~) very tired.

Das Wichtigste in Kürze

■ Gebrauch: 1. „Hintergrund-Situation", die unterbrochen wurde; 2. vorübergehend andauernde Situation
■ Keine Verlaufsform bei Zustandsverben

Weitere Informationen → Unit 14

A One sentence has a mistake. Which sentence is correct?

a I didn't go to work yesterday. ✔
b I wasn't going to work yesterday.

1 **a** Dave arrived when I was washing up.
b Dave arrived when I washed up.

2 **a** Did the children wait when you got home?
b Were the children waiting when you got home?

3 **a** I tried to call you at six. What did you do?
b I tried to call you at six. What were you doing?

4 **a** When I was a child, I wanted to be a nurse.
b When I was a child, I was wanting to be a nurse.

5 **a** Julie was falling downstairs last week.
b Julie fell downstairs last week.

6 **a** Sorry, I wasn't listening. What did you say?
b Sorry, I didn't listen. What did you say?

B Make questions and answers.

What / you / do / when the children / come home? – I / watch TV.
What were you doing when the children came home? – I was watching TV.

1 Which country / the president / visit / when he / become ill? – He / visit Spain.
2 How fast / they / drive / when the accident / happen? – They / drive at 120 km an hour.
3 What / Helen / do / when she / meet her husband? – She / do research for her new book.
4 Who / John / speak to / when the secretary / walk in? – He / speak to his boss.
5 Where / the children / play / when the dog / attack them? – They / play in the park.

C Complete these dialogues with the verbs in the simple past or the past continuous.

A: Guess who I *met* (meet) when I *was standing* (stand) at the bus stop.
B: No idea. Who *did you meet* (you/meet)?

1 A: .... (it/rain) when you .... (leave) home this morning?
B: Yes, but when I .... (get) to work the sun .... (shine).

2 A: Why .... (you/switch) the television off?
B: Nobody .... (watch) it and I .... (want) to read.

3 A: .... (you/phone) the travel agent's yesterday?
B: No, I'm afraid I .... (forget). I .... (remember) when I .... (wait) for the bus but then it was too late.

4 A: Where .... (you/go) when I .... (see) you yesterday afternoon? You .... (seem) to be in a hurry.
B: I was. I .... (go) to Sue's wedding. That's why I .... (wear) that funny hat.

5 A: The tour guide .... (give) us an interesting leaflet about the church this morning.
B: Did she? I missed that because I .... (go) to the bank. When I .... (come) back, she .... (talk) about the castle.

D Translate the following sentences.

1 Als der Lehrer in das Klassenzimmer kam, spielten die Kinder mit einem Ball.
2 Ich habe dich um elf angerufen. Wo warst du? – Ich saß im Garten und habe das Telefon nicht gehört.
3 Hast du Jill gestern gesehen? – Ja, sie sah furchtbar aus. Sie trug ein schreckliches grünes Kleid.
4 Als wir in London ankamen, regnete es und wir wollten wieder nachhause fahren.
5 Letzte Woche um diese Zeit lag ich am Strand.

7 Present perfect

A: Have you seen that new film at the Odeon yet?
B: Yes, it's good. I ~~was in~~ *have been to* the cinema a lot ~~in the last time~~ *recently*.
A: Really? I thought you were a sports person, a tennis fan.
B: Yes, but I ~~had~~ *have had* only one or two games lately.
A: Well, how about a game this weekend?
B: OK. ~~Were you ever in~~ *Have you ever been to* the new sports centre? I hear it's very good.

Form

■ **have** oder **has** + Partizip Perfekt	Sally **has moved**. They**'ve bought** a flat in town. *Sally ist umgezogen. Sie haben eine Wohnung in der Stadt gekauft.*
■ Form des Partizips: regelmäßige Verben*: wie Vergangenheitsform	I**'ve booked** a table. *Ich habe einen Tisch reserviert.*
unregelmäßige Verben: besondere Formen (s.u.)	Tom **has sent** a card. The Wilsons **have written** too. *Tom hat eine Karte geschickt. Die Wilsons haben auch geschrieben.*
■ Verneinung: **have/has** + **not**	I **haven't slept**. Tony **hasn't come** home. *Ich habe nicht geschlafen. Tony ist nicht nach Hause gekommen.*
■ Fragen, Kurzantworten: **have/has**	**Have** you **phoned**? – Yes, I **have**. / No, I **haven't**. *Hast du angerufen? – Ja./Nein.* **Has** Ed **come**? – Yes, he **has**. / No, he **hasn't**. *Ist Ed gekommen? – Ja./Nein.*

*Schreibbesonderheiten: siehe Seite 111

Unregelmäßige Verben (vollständige Liste siehe Umschlagklappe/Lesezeichen)

be	was/were	**been**	go	went	**gone**	run	ran	**run**
buy	bought	**bought**	have	had	**had**	say	said	**said**
come	came	**come**	know	knew	**known**	see	saw	**seen**
do	did	**done**	make	made	**made**	tell	told	**told**
get	got	**got**	meet	met	**met**	take	took	**taken**
give	gave	**given**	read	read	**read**	write	wrote	**written**

Gebrauch und Signalwörter

! Mit dem Present Perfect wird ausgedrückt, dass etwas – irgendwann – in der Zeit bis jetzt geschehen ist. Der Zeitpunkt ist entweder unwichtig oder unbekannt; im Vordergrund steht allein die Tatsache, dass etwas geschehen ist. Wird der Zeitpunkt genannt, darf das Present Perfect nicht gebraucht werden!

■ Typische Signalwörter sind Ausdrücke für die ganze Zeit bis jetzt sowie für die (aller)letzte Zeit.

die ganze Zeit bis jetzt	already *(schon)*, yet? *(schon* – in Fragen*)*, before *(schon einmal)*, so far *(bisher)*, always *(schon immer)*, ever? *(je? schon einmal?)*, never *(nie)*, not yet *(noch nicht)*
die (aller)letzte Zeit	just *(gerade)*, recently *(in letzter Zeit)*, lately *(in letzter Zeit)*

■ Stellung: **so far**, **before**, **yet**, **recently**, **lately** stehen am Satzende, andere Ausdrücke vor dem Partizip.
I**'ve met** Ann **before**, but I **haven't met** Tom **yet**. I**'ve never been** to Rome. **Have** you **ever been** there?

Das Wichtigste in Kürze

■ Regelmäßige Verben: **have/has** + **-ed**; unregelmäßige Verben: besondere Formen
■ Das Present Perfect ist nicht möglich, wenn ein fester Zeitpunkt genannt wird

Weitere Informationen → Units 8-10
Zu amerikanischem Gebrauch → Seite 103

A One sentence has a mistake. Which sentence is correct?

a I never have read this book.
b I have never read this book. ✔

1 **a** Have you ever been to Italy?
b Were you ever in Italy?

2 **a** He has done already his homework.
b He has already done his homework.

3 **a** Have you written to Sue in the last time?
b Have you written to Sue lately?

4 **a** Joy have not phoned yet.
b Joy has not phoned yet.

5 **a** Pete isn't here. He is gone to the bank.
b Pete isn't here. He has gone to the bank.

6 **a** I've been to Finland before.
b I've been in Finland before.

B Make complete sentences.

(never) I / be / Canada *I've never been to Canada.*

1 (before) Paul / be / the USA
2 (ever) your son / run away from home?
3 (just) I / finish my homework
4 (yet) you / do your homework?
5 (always) we / want to go to Israel
6 (recently) I / have a lot of work

C Complete these dialogues with the verbs in the correct form.

A: Let's go to the opera tomorrow.
B: That's a good idea. I *haven't been* (not be) to the opera lately.

1 A: What's the matter with Tom?
B: He .... (just hear) some bad news.

2 A: What's the new Chinese restaurant like?
B: I don't know. I .... (not be) there yet.

3 A: Are the children at home or .... (they/go out)?
B: I'm afraid you .... (just miss) them. They .... (go) to the cinema.

4 A: .... (your husband/give up) smoking yet?
B: No, he .... (have) a lot of problems.

D Give short answers.

Have you booked a table? – Yes, *I have.*

1 Has Craig invited you to his party? –
No, ...

2 Have you heard from Ann? –
Yes, ...

3 Have the children done their homework yet? –
No, ...

4 Has Sue phoned recently? –
Yes, ...

E Write questions for these answers.

A: *Have you ever been* to Wales?
B: Wales? No, I haven't but I'd love to go.

1 A: How many people .... ?
B: I've invited twenty.

2 A: How many books .... ?
B: John Grisham? He's written several.

3 A: .... where to go on holiday?
B: No, we haven't decided yet.

4 A: .... to the cinema recently?
B: No, I've been far too busy.

5 A: .... to Berlin?
B: Yes, we have – it's a great city.

8 Present perfect – Simple past (1)
Present Perfect – Einfache Vergangenheit (1)

A: Ann and I ~~have seen~~ saw the new Spielberg film yesterday.
B: Was it good?
A: Yes, but the book is better. I ~~have read~~ read it on holiday.
B: You've been to the cinema a lot recently.
A: Yes, I ~~was~~ have been there three times so far this month.
B: I know! You went with me last week.

Present Perfect

- Mit dem Present Perfect wird ausgedrückt, dass etwas irgendwann in der Zeit bis zur Gegenwart geschehen ist.
  I **have been** to the USA. ⇢
  Tom says he **has seen** this film before. ⇢

Einfache Vergangenheit

- Mit der einfachen Vergangenheit wird ausgedrückt, dass etwas zu einem bestimmten Zeitpunkt in der Vergangenheit abgeschlossen wurde.
  I **went** there in 1999.
  He **saw** it on RTL a few months ago.

- In Fragen wird oft gefragt, ob etwas überhaupt (d.h. in der ganzen Zeit bis jetzt) geschehen ist.
  Have you ever **been** to Australia? – Yes, I have. ⇢
  Has Tom **phoned**? – Yes, he has. ⇢

- In Fragen wird oft gefragt, wann (d.h. zu welchem vergangenen Zeitpunkt) etwas geschehen ist.
  When **did** you **go** there?
  When **did** he **ring**?

- In zusammenhängenden Texten wird oft mit dem Present Perfect zunächst die „nackte" Tatsache festgestellt, dass etwas geschehen ist, ohne dass die näheren Umstände (insbesondere der Zeitpunkt) genannt werden. Weitere Einzelheiten zu Hintergrund und Hergang folgen in der einfachen Vergangenheit.
  I'**ve been** to Chile. ⇢ Really? Where **did** you **go**? What **did** you **see**?
  John **has broken** his arm. ⇢ He **fell** off his bike yesterday.
  I'**ve lost** my watch. ⇢ It **happened** yesterday evening somewhere in town.

Present Perfect und einfache Vergangenheit mit und ohne Zeitangaben

- Beide Zeitformen werden mit typischen Signalwörtern gebraucht (siehe Units 5 und 7). In Sätzen mit der einfachen Vergangenheit wird dabei ein bestimmter Zeitpunkt genannt.
  I **have visited** Italy **before**. ⇢ We **spent** our holidays there again **last year**.
  I **have seen** the film *Casablanca* 15 times **so far**. ⇢ I first **saw** it when I **was** a teenager **20 years ago**.

! Auch wenn kein Zeitpunkt genannt wird, muss die einfache Vergangenheit gebraucht werden, wenn sich das Geschehen zu einem ganz bestimmten Zeitpunkt in der Vergangenheit ereignet haben muss.
  Workers **have found** a 2000-year-old building. ⇢ The Romans **built** it. This place **was** a Roman town.
  Sheila **has lived** in lots of different countries. ⇢ She **was born** in New Zealand.
  I **have read** *Hamlet*. ⇢ It's one of the most famous plays Shakespeare **wrote**.

Gegenwartsbezug des Present Perfect

- Mit dem Present Perfect wird oft ein Geschehen genannt, das in irgendeiner Form Auswirkungen auf die Gegenwart hat (deshalb auch der Name *Present* Perfect).
  I'**ve been** to Scotland. [= Ich kenne Schottland.]
  They'**ve closed** the road! [= Wir müssen jetzt einen Umweg fahren.]

Das Wichtigste in Kürze

- Present Perfect nicht möglich, wenn ein bestimmter Zeitpunkt genannt oder gedacht wird
- Present Perfect: etwas hat sich irgendwann ereignet und hat jetzt Auswirkungen, ist jetzt wichtig/relevant

Weitere Informationen ⇢ Unit 10
Zu amerikanischem Gebrauch ⇢ Seite 103

A One sentence has a mistake. Which sentence is correct?

a Ben broke his leg last week. ✔
b Ben has broken his leg last week.

1 a The Berlin Wall fell in 1989.
b The Berlin Wall has fallen in 1989.

2 a Jackie had an accident two weeks ago.
b Jackie has had an accident two weeks ago.

3 a I didn't have time to go to the bank yesterday.
b I haven't had time to go to the bank yesterday.

4 a Sorry, I've forgotten to phone you last night.
b Sorry, I forgot to phone you last night.

5 a When have you bought your new coat?
b When did you buy your new coat?

6 a I was in LA several times – it's a great city.
b I've been to LA several times – it's a great city.

B Make dialogues as in the example.

A: you / ever / work in the USA? *Have you ever worked in the USA?*
B: Yes, I / work in New York in 1998. *Yes, I worked in New York in 1998.*

1 A: you / ever / break your arm or your leg?
B: Yes, I / break my leg three years ago.

2 A: you / read Robert Goddard's latest book?
B: Yes, I / read it while I was on holiday.

3 A: you / find your keys yet?
B: Yes, I / find them a few minutes ago.

4 A: you / do your homework yet?
B: Yes, I / do it yesterday.

C Complete these dialogues with the verbs in the present perfect or simple past.

A: I *went* (go) to the Monet exhibition yesterday. *Have you seen* (you/see) it yet?
B: No, I *wanted* (want) to go last week but there *were* (be) so many people.

1 A: .... (you/speak) to Dave yet?
B: No. I .... (phone) him at 2 o'clock and I .... (ring) again at three o'clock but he .... (not be) at home.

2 A: .... (you/learn) French when you were at school?
B: Yes, but that .... (be) 20 years ago and now I .... (forget) most of it. I .... (not like) the French teacher and so I .... (not do) my homework.

3 A: We .... (just book) our summer holidays. What about you?
B: Well, we .... (get) some brochures from the travel agency last week, but we still .... (not decide) where to go.

4 A: Last week I .... (decide) to go on a diet. I .... (buy) a new suit a couple of months ago and now it doesn't fit. I .... (never wear) it!
B: I .... (try) to lose weight last year but I .... (not be) very successful – I .... (give up) after a month.

D Translate the following sentences.

1 John hat ein neues Auto gekauft. Er hat es letzte Woche gekauft. Es war nicht teuer.
2 Du kannst das Buch haben. Ich habe es gelesen. Ich habe es im Urlaub gelesen; es war sehr gut.
3 Hast du alle Einladungen geschrieben? – Nein, gestern habe ich nur zehn geschrieben.
4 Hat Sandra uns ihre neue Telefonnummer gegeben? – Nein. Sie hat uns letzte Woche eine Postkarte geschickt, aber sie hat die neue Nummer vergessen.
5 Habt ihr von Hilary und George gehört? Sie sind umgezogen! – Tatsächlich? Wann sind sie umgezogen?

9 Present perfect with "since" and "for"
Present Perfect mit „since" und „for"

A: How long ~~do you know~~ have you known Claire?
B: Oh, a long time. She's nice, isn't she?
A: Yes, her brother's nice too. I ~~know him since~~ have known him for three years.
B: Oh really? He's still on holiday in the USA at the moment, isn't he?
A: Well, ~~he's~~ he has been there all summer, but he's coming back next week.
B: I see.

Bedeutungsunterschied since – for (beide „seit")

- **Mit since benennt man den Anfangszeitpunkt, an dem etwas begonnen hat.**
  since = „seit" + Zeitpunkt
  since 1999, since 4 o'clock, since yesterday morning, since Tuesday, since last year

- **Mit for nennt man eine Zeitspanne und sagt, wie lange etwas andauert.**
  for = „seit" + Zeitspanne
  for five minutes, for two hours, for six weeks, for a month, for years, for ages *(seit Ewigkeiten)*

Gebrauch

Mit since und for + Present Perfect wird ausgedrückt, dass etwas in der Vergangenheit begonnen hat und bis in die Gegenwart andauert. Das Verb steht nicht – wie im Deutschen – in der Gegenwart!

They've had (~~They have~~) snow since last Monday.
Sie haben seit letztem Montag Schnee.
We've known (~~We know~~) Sam since 1990.
Wir kennen Sam seit 1990.
I've been (~~I am~~)here since 9 o'clock.
Ich bin seit 9 Uhr hier.

They've had (~~They have~~) snow for ten days now.
Sie haben jetzt seit zehn Tagen Schnee.
We've known (~~We know~~) Sam for over ten years.
Wir kennen Sam seit über zehn Jahren.
It's 11 now, so I've been (~~I am~~) here for two hours.
Es ist jetzt 11, also bin ich seit zwei Stunden hier.

- **Auch in Fragen mit How long? und bei Zeitangaben mit all wird das Present Perfect gebraucht, wenn ein Zeitraum bis zur Gegenwart gemeint ist.**
  How long have you been a professional? *Seit wann / Wie lange sind Sie (schon) Profi?*
  How long have you known each other? *Wie lange kennen Sie sich (schon)?*
  We've had no electricity all day. *Wir haben schon den ganzen Tag (lang) keinen Strom.*
  Tom has been ill all week. *Tom ist schon die ganze Woche (lang) krank.*

- **Generell gilt im Englischen, dass das Present Perfect gebraucht werden muss, wenn ein in der Vergangenheit begonnener Zustand bis in die Gegenwart andauert.**
  They have always wanted to buy a house. *Sie wollten schon immer ein Haus kaufen.*
  We haven't had time to discuss this. *Wir hatten keine Zeit, um dieses zu besprechen.*

Das Wichtigste in Kürze

- **„seit" = since + Zeitpunkt, for + Zeitspanne**
- **since/for steht mit dem Present Perfect, nicht mit der einfachen Form / Verlaufsform der Gegenwart**

Weitere Informationen → Unit 10

A One sentence has a mistake. Which sentence is correct?

a We've been married since June. ✔
b We are married since June.

1 a How long do you know Ken?
b How long have you known Ken?

2 a Jane has been here since two weeks.
b Jane has been here for two weeks.

3 a I have a headache all morning.
b I've had a headache all morning.

4 a How long have you this car?
b How long have you had this car?

5 a We know each other since our school days.
b We've known each other since our school days.

6 a I've always wanted to go to LA – next year maybe.
b I always wanted to go to LA – next year maybe.

B Since or for?

I've lived here *since* I was born.

1 They've been married .... 1992.

2 We've known each other .... ages.

3 Alan has had visitors .... last week.

4 Angela has been in Wales .... the end of June.

5 I haven't felt well .... I got up.

6 We haven't had a holiday .... two years.

C Complete these dialogues with the verbs in the correct form and choose since or for.

A: How long *have you been married* (you/be married)?
B: ~~Since~~/For two years, but *we've known* (know) each other since/~~for~~ 1996.

1 A: .... (you/meet) Carol before?

B: Yes, we .... (know) each other since/for we were students, but we .... (not see) each other since/for years.

2 A: How long .... (your son/be) in France?

B: Since/For the beginning of the month. He .... (only write) once so far.

3 A: I .... (not hear) from Barry and Julie since/for their party. .... (you/see) them recently?

B: Julie .... (be) away twice this month. I .... (not speak) to her since/for several days now.

4 A: I .... (always want) to go to New Zealand. .... (you/ever be) there?

B: No, I haven't. Actually, I .... (not have) a real holiday since/for a long time.

5 A: How long .... (you/be) with this company?

B: Too long! I .... (be) here since/for I left school. I .... (never have) another job.

D Translate the following sentences.

1 Wir sind jetzt in Spanien. Wir sind seit einer Woche hier.
2 Ich habe schon den ganzen Tag Probleme mit meinem Computer. Ich habe einen sehr alten Computer.
3 Wie lange ist dein Sohn schon in Österreich? Ist er in Salzburg oder Wien?
4 Ich kenne Mary schon mein ganzes Leben lang. Wir sehen uns jeden Monat.
5 Wie lange kennst du deinen Mann? – Wir kennen uns schon lange, aber wir sind erst seit zwei Monaten verheiratet. Wir sind sehr glücklich.

10 Present perfect – Simple past (2)
Present Perfect – Einfache Vergangenheit (2)

A: Four o'clock at last. What a day!
B: ~~I've had~~ I had a terrible morning and I ~~have~~ have had a headache all afternoon.
A: I've had an awful day too.
B: This morning I ~~have missed~~ missed the bus.
A: I've been so busy. No time for coffee, lunch – nothing.
B: ~~I've had~~ I had a sandwich at lunchtime, but that's all.

Present Perfect und einfache Vergangenheit mit den gleichen Zeitangaben

- **Zeitangaben mit for können unterschiedliche Bedeutung haben. Wenn mit for ein Zeitraum bis zur Gegenwart gemeint ist, wird das Present Perfect gebraucht.**
  Ist ein abgeschlossener Zeitraum gemeint, steht das Verb in der einfachen Vergangenheit.

Andy is ill. He has had the flu for 2 weeks. → Tim is fit again. He was ill for 2 weeks.
Andy ist krank. Er hat seit 2 Wochen die Grippe. *Tim ist wieder fit. Er war 2 Wochen lang krank.*
I've been a member of the tennis club for 3 years. → Before that I was in a football club for 3 years.
Ich bin seit 3 Jahren Mitglied in diesem Tennisklub. *Davor war ich 3 Jahre (lang) in einem Fußballverein.*

- **Auch always, never, all können sich auf die ganze Zeit bis zur Gegenwart (Present Perfect) oder auf einen in der Vergangenheit abgeschlossenen Zeitraum (einfache Vergangenheit) beziehen.**

I have always loved the cinema. → As a child I always went to the cinema on Sunday.
Ich habe das Kino schon immer geliebt. *Als Kind bin ich immer sonntags ins Kino gegangen.*
I've never been to Canada. → When I lived in the USA I never had time.
Ich war noch nie in Kanada. *Als ich in den USA lebte, hatte ich nie Zeit.*
I've had earache all day. → I had it all day yesterday too.
Ich habe schon den ganzen Tag Ohrenschmerzen. *Ich hatte gestern auch den ganzen Tag welche.*

- **Auch Zeitangaben mit this ... und today können mit dem Present Perfect oder der einfachen Vergangenheit gebraucht werden. Ist der Zeitraum abgeschlossen, muss die einfache Vergangenheit gebraucht werden.**

(morgens, 11 Uhr) I've spoken to Bill this morning. *(ab Mittag)* I spoke to Bill this morning.
(16 Uhr) We've been swimming this afternoon. *(20 Uhr)* We went swimming this afternoon.

Zusammenfassung (Units 8-10)

Present Perfect

1 **Die Handlung/Situation ist nicht abgeschlossen.**
We've been here for 15 years.

2 **Eine Serie wiederholter Handlungen ist noch nicht abgeschlossen.**
Watson has played for England 54 times so far.

3 **Die Handlung ist irgendwann in der Zeit bis zur Gegenwart geschehen.**
I've been to Norway.

4 **Die Handlung ist noch relevant/aktuell, hat noch Auswirkungen in der Gegenwart.**
I've lost my wallet. What can I do?

Einfache Vergangenheit

1 **Die Handlung/Situation ist abgeschlossen.**
We moved here from Oxford.

2 **Eine Serie wiederholter Handlungen wurde in der Vergangenheit abgeschlossen.**
Bond played for Wales 77 times. He died last week.

2 **Die Handlung geschah zu einem bestimmten Zeitpunkt in der Vergangenheit.**
I went in 1997. It was in the summer.

4 **Die Handlung gehört der Vergangenheit an und hat keine Folgen in der Gegenwart.**
I lost my passport once, but I got it back again.

Das Wichtigste in Kürze

- Einfache Vergangenheit: in der Vergangenheit abgeschlossen, beendet
- Present Perfect: nicht abgeschlossen, oder aber irgendwann geschehen und jetzt noch relevant und aktuell

Zu amerikanischem Gebrauch siehe Seite 103

A One sentence has a mistake. Which sentence is correct?

a We lived in Boston for two years – from 1982–1984. ✔
b We've lived in Boston for two years – from 1982–1984.

1 a How many plays has Shakespeare written?
b How many plays did Shakespeare write?

2 a When I was a student, I worked on a farm.
b When I was a student, I have worked on a farm.

3 a My uncle died when I was ten. I never met him.
b My uncle died when I was ten. I've never met him.

4 a As children, we have always had a dog.
b As children, we always had a dog.

5 a I've lost my car keys yesterday.
b I lost my car keys yesterday.

6 a I've been here for two weeks – I leave next week.
b I was here for two weeks – I leave next week.

B Present perfect or simple past?

(It's 6 pm.) I didn't have (not have) breakfast today.

1 *(It's June.)* We .... (not have) a holiday this year.

2 *(It's 11 am.)* My alarm clock .... (not ring) this morning and I was late.

3 *(It's December.)* We .... (not have) much snow so far this winter.

4 *(It's Thursday.)* Harry .... (be) late for work every morning this week.

5 *(It's Saturday evening.)* I .... (not see) the neighbours this weekend. Are they away?

C Complete these dialogues with the verbs in the present perfect or simple past.

1 A: My goodness! It's 11 o'clock and I still .... (not have) breakfast.
I .... (have) a coffee when I .... (get up) – that's all.
B: Let's go for lunch soon. A new bistro .... (open) last month – it's great.

2 A: What a week! I .... (work) all day yesterday without a break and I
.... (not have) a break today either. Still, only one more hour!
B: I .... (make) some sandwiches this morning – would you like one?

3 A: I'm sorry to hear about your grandfather. When .... (he/die)?
B: Well, he .... (be) ill for a long time and then three weeks ago he
.... (go) into hospital and .... (die) two days later.
Since then my grandmother .... (be) with my parents.

4 A: I .... (decide) to go to Scotland this year – next month probably.
.... (you/ever be) there?
B: Yes, once as a child. My grandparents .... (take) me there.
It really .... (be) a wonderful holiday.

D Translate the following sentences.

1 Es ist 15.00 Uhr und ich habe den ganzen Tag nichts getan. Gestern habe ich den ganzen Tag nur im Garten gesessen.
2 Vor zwanzig Jahren haben wir *Hamlet* in der Schule gelesen und gestern habe ich das Stück (*play*) im Theater gesehen.
3 Mein Mann ist seit einer Woche im Krankenhaus. Letztes Jahr war er auch im Krankenhaus.
4 Es ist schon Dienstag und meine Tochter hat immer noch nicht angerufen. Am Samstag ist sie nach Rom geflogen und hat versprochen anzurufen.

11 Present perfect continuous (1)
Verlaufsform des Present Perfect (1)

A: How long ~~are you living~~ have you been living here now, Andrew?
B: Over ten years. We came when Sally got a job at the new hospital.
A: ~~I've been knowing~~ I've known her for a long time, but I never realized that she once worked at the hospital.
B: Well, she didn't like it much. That's why she changed to the university.
A: She ~~works~~ has been working there since Jack and I came here.

Form

- have/has been ...ing — I've been reading. Sue has been working.
- Verneinung, Fragen wie Present Perfect (Unit 7) — We haven't been watching TV. Have you been looking for us? – Yes, I have.

Gebrauch

- Die Verlaufsform des Present Perfect drückt aus, dass etwas in der Vergangenheit begonnen hat und bis in die Gegenwart andauert.
  Mit since nennt man den Anfangszeitpunkt, mit for die Zeitspanne, die eine Handlung schon andauert.

Tom has been sitting (~~Tom is sitting~~) here since 9 o'clock. *Tom sitzt hier seit 9 Uhr.*
We've been waiting (~~We are waiting~~) for an hour. *Wir warten seit einer Stunde.*
I've been living and working (~~I live and work~~) here since 1995. *Ich wohne und arbeite hier seit 1995.*
Is she ill? She has been eating (~~She is eating~~) so little recently. *... Sie isst so wenig in letzter Zeit.*

! Im Gegensatz zum deutschen Sprachgebrauch kann das Verb nicht in der Gegenwart stehen (siehe Unit 9).

Gebrauchsunterschied zwischen Verlaufsform und einfacher Form des Present Perfect

- Bei bestimmten Verben (z.B. live, work) kann man beide Formen ohne Unterschied gebrauchen.
  I have been living here for a long time. / I have lived here for a long time. *Ich wohne schon lange hier.*
  Ed has been working for IBM since 1999. / Ed has worked for IBM since 1999. *Ed arbeitet seit 1999 bei IBM.*

! Die Verlaufsform ist nicht möglich bei Zustandsverben wie know, have usw. (siehe Units 4 und 9).
~~I have been knowing Janet for 10 years.~~ I have known Janet for 10 years. *Ich kenne Janet seit 10 Jahren.*
~~I have been having this cold for a week.~~ I have had this cold for a week. *Ich bin seit einer Woche erkältet.*

- Die Verlaufsform ist nicht möglich, wenn mit always über die ganze Zeit bis jetzt gesprochen wird.
  ~~I've always been driving a Ford~~. I've always driven a Ford. *Ich fahre schon immer Ford.*

Das Wichtigste in Kürze

- Verlaufsform des Present Perfect, nicht Gegenwart, wenn etwas bis jetzt andauert
- „seit": since (+ Anfangszeitpunkt) oder for (+ Zeitspanne)
- Zustandsverben und always (= ganze Zeit bis jetzt): einfache Form (nicht Verlaufsform) des Present Perfect

Weitere Informationen → Units 12,14

A One sentence has a mistake. Which sentence is correct?

a John is living here since 1998.
b John has been living here since 1998. ✔

1 **a** I have been working at this bank since 14 years.
b I have been working at this bank for 14 years.

2 **a** Sorry, I'm late. Are you waiting long?
b Sorry, I'm late. Have you been waiting long?

3 **a** How long has Jane been living in the USA?
b How long does Jane live in the USA?

4 **a** Have your parents always been living in Bristol?
b Have your parents always lived in Bristol?

5 **a** We've known each other for years.
b We've been knowing each other for years.

6 **a** I'm so tired! I do a lot of overtime recently.
b I'm so tired! I've been doing a lot of overtime recently.

B Ask questions with How long ...? and the present perfect continuous. Give answers with for or since.

A: you / live in Berlin? *How long have you been living in Berlin?*
B: five years *For five years.*

1 A: you / wait?
B: 20 minutes

2 A: your wife / learn French?
B: last October

3 A: your children / travel round Europe?
B: the beginning of the summer holidays

4 A: you / look for a new flat?
B: ages

5 A: it / snow?
B: I got up

C Complete these dialogues with the verbs in the correct form. Use the present perfect continuous where possible.

A: How's the weather in Spain?
B: Terrible! It'*s been raining* (rain) since we arrived.

1 A: Is your son still in Australia?
B: Yes, he .... (work) there since he left university.

2 A: Time goes so quickly! Do you realize Sam and I .... (live) here for over ten years now?
B: I know. We .... (be) here since we got married.

3 A: How long .... (you/look for) a new job?
B: Since May. I .... (know) since then that the firm will probably close down.

4 A: What's the matter? You .... (stare) out of the window for ages.
B: I .... (think about) my mother. She .... (be) in hospital since last Wednesday.
A: I didn't realize she wasn't well. How long .... (she/be) ill?

5 A: Where have you been? I .... (wait) for over 30 minutes!
B: I'm sorry. I .... (try) to reach you on your mobile phone since I left work.
A: Typical! I .... (have) the phone for two months now and nobody ever phones me so I left it at home.

D Translate the following sentences.

1 Wir wohnen in Leipzig. Wir wohnen dort seit sieben Jahren.
2 Kennst du Harry? – Ja, wir kennen uns seit Jahren.
3 Ich habe Kopfschmerzen. Ich habe seit drei Tagen Kopfschmerzen.
4 Ich arbeite in der Exportabteilung. Wie lange arbeiten Sie schon hier?
5 Mein Mann arbeitet immer hart, aber in der letzten Zeit arbeitet er zu viel.

12 Present perfect continuous (2)
Verlaufsform des Present Perfect (2)

A: Why are you so dirty? Just look at your face and clothes!
B: ~~I've painted.~~ I've been painting.
A: I can see that, but what? You've got paint everywhere!
B: Jane's flat. ~~We've painted~~ We've been painting her flat all afternoon.
A: All of it, in one afternoon?
B: No, no. ~~We've been managing~~ We've managed one room. We're going to do the other two tomorrow.

Gebrauch bei abgeschlossenen Handlungen

- **In Unit 11 wurde festgestellt, dass mit der Verlaufsform des Present Perfect etwas ausgedrückt wird, das in der Vergangenheit begonnen hat und bis in die Gegenwart andauert.**
  Die Handlung / Der Vorgang kann aber auch – meist kurz vorher – beendet worden sein.
  Where have you been? – I've been helping Jane. *Wo bist du gewesen? – Ich habe Jane geholfen.*
  What a day! I've been painting the kitchen. *Was für ein Tag! Ich habe die Küche gestrichen.*

- **Oft hat der abgeschlossene Vorgang noch unmittelbare – vielleicht sichtbare – Folgen.**
  Der Sprecher erklärt die Gründe für die gegenwärtige Situation.
  You're out of breath. – Yes, I've been running. *Du bist außer Atem. – Ja, ich bin gelaufen.*
  Why is your hair wet? – I've been swimming. *Warum sind deine Haare nass? – Ich war schwimmen.*

Gebrauchsunterschied zwischen Verlaufsform und einfacher Form bei abgeschlossenen Handlungen

- **Die Verlaufsform betont die Handlung und deren Andauern, die einfache Form drückt das Endergebnis aus.**

I need to wash. I've been painting my bedroom. →	I've painted my bedroom. I'll paint the kitchen now.
You look tired. – I've been reading reports. →	I've read six long reports.
We've been writing Christmas cards. →	We've written to our relatives, but not to our friends.

- **Die Verlaufsform ist nicht möglich, wenn ein Ergebnis (Frage „wie viel/viele") genannt wird.**

~~We've been taking over 100 photos.~~	We've taken over 100 photos.
~~Ann has been reading 300 pages.~~	Ann has read 300 pages.
~~How many potatoes has he been eating?~~	How many potatoes has he eaten?

- **Die einfache Form ist meist nicht möglich, wenn nur gesagt wird, mit welcher Art von Tätigkeit sich jemand beschäftigt hat. Dies ist oft der Fall in Sätzen ohne Objekt.**

Where have you been? – I've been working outside.	~~I've worked outside.~~
Have you been busy? – Yes, I've been cooking.	~~Yes, I've cooked.~~

Das Wichtigste in Kürze

- Verlaufsform des Present Perfect, wenn etwas kurz zuvor abgeschlossen wurde und noch nachwirkt
- Verlaufsform betont Handlung und Andauern; einfache Form betont Endergebnis
- Antwort auf Frage „wie viel/viele": einfache Form
- Reine Angabe zur Tätigkeit: Verlaufsform

Weitere Informationen → Unit 14

A One sentence has a mistake. Which sentence is correct?

a I've called Sue six times today – she's never at home. ✔
b I've been calling Sue six times today – she's never at home.

1 a I've been reading a great book. I'll soon finish it.
b I've read a great book. I'll soon finish it.

2 a How much has Jo been saving for her holiday?
b How much has Jo saved for her holiday?

3 a I've done 40 hours overtime this month.
b I've been doing 40 hours overtime this month.

4 a Gary's exhausted. He's jogged.
b Gary's exhausted. He's been jogging.

5 a We've been trying to call all day. Where can he be?
b We try to call all day. Where can he be?

6 a I've written ten cards since breakfast.
b I've been writing ten cards since breakfast.

B Present perfect or present perfect continuous?

I*'ve been reading* (read) this book for two hours. I*'ve read* (read) four chapters so far.

1 So far I .... (teach) at four schools in Munich.
I .... (be) at this school since 1999.

2 How long .... (Jenny/learn) to drive?
How many driving lessons .... (she/have) so far?

3 Janet .... (talk) to her friend on the phone for 45 minutes now.
She .... (make) six calls since she got home from school!

4 Jack's wet and dirty because he .... (wash) the car.
He .... (wash) it twice this month.

C Complete these sentences with the verbs in the correct form: present continuous, present perfect or present perfect continuous.

1 build They .... a new shopping complex at the moment.
They .... it ever since we moved here.
They .... about half of it so far.

2 write I've got a new hobby – I .... a cookery book.
I .... the main part of the book. I finished it last week.
I .... the introduction since then.

3 cut We .... all the hedges in the garden – they look much better.
At the moment my wife .... the lawn.
I .... the rose bushes all morning and still haven't finished.

4 read I .... ever since I got up.
I .... a great book at the moment – it was a birthday present.
It's so good – I .... three quarters of it already.

5 play My daughter .... at several important concerts.
Listen! She .... a piece by Chopin.
She .... the piano since she was a child.

D Complete these dialogues with the verbs in the correct form: simple present, present perfect or present perfect continuous.

1 A: Don't come in the house – you're really dirty! What .... (you/do)?
B: I .... (help) dad clean the garage.

2 A: Where .... (you/be)? I .... (not see) you all afternoon.
B: I .... (watch) television.

3 A: Congratulations on your new job! .... (you/like) it?
B: I .... (only be) there for a few days but it .... (seem) fine.

4 A: The phone .... (be) engaged for hours! Who .... (you/speak) to?
B: Margaret. She .... (want) us to go for dinner on Saturday.

13 Past perfect
Vollendete Vergangenheit

A: Sorry I'm late. My train was late because of the snow.
B: I was lucky. When I left home, they ~~already cleared~~ had already cleared the roads.
A: Is there any coffee?
B: There should be. When I looked in the kitchen a few minutes ago, someone ~~has just put~~ had just put the machine on.
A: Good. My feet are like ice. I need something hot to warm me up.
B: Like Jane. Her bus was very late. When it finally arrived, she ~~was waiting~~ had been waiting in the cold for over 40 minutes.

Form

- **Einfache Form: had(n't) + Partizip Perfekt** — I arrived at 5.00. By (*Bis*) 6.30 I had unpacked. I had had a shower. I hadn't eaten. Had you phoned home? – Yes, I had. / No, I hadn't.
- **Verlaufsform: had(n't) been ...ing** — When the bus came, I had been waiting for 3 minutes. I hadn't been waiting long. Had you been hurrying? – Yes, I had. / No, I hadn't.

Gebrauch

- **Mit dem Past Perfect wird ausgedrückt, dass etwas vor einem vergangenen Zeitpunkt abgeschlossen wurde.**

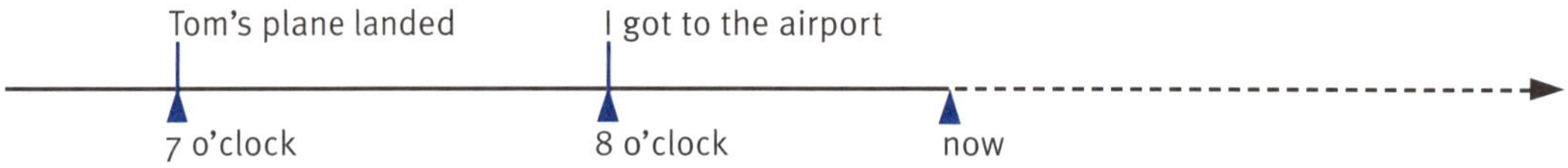

When I got to the airport, Tom's plane had already landed.

- **Die Verlaufsform des Past Perfect drückt aus, dass etwas vor einem vergangenen Zeitpunkt angefangen hatte und bis zu diesem Zeitpunkt andauerte. Die Dauer wird oft mit for oder since angegeben.**
  He had been waiting for a whole hour / since 8 o'clock. *Er wartete schon eine ganze Stunde / seit 8 Uhr.*

! **Bei Zustandsverben ist die Verlaufsform nicht möglich (siehe Liste Unit 4).**
I hadn't known (~~hadn't been knowing~~) that he would take an earlier flight.

Gebrauchsunterschiede: Past Perfect Verlaufsform / Einfache Form – Einfache Vergangenheit

- **Die Verlaufsform betont die Handlung und deren Andauern, die einfache Form drückt das Endergebnis aus. Die Verlaufsform ist nicht möglich, wenn ein Ergebnis (Frage „wie viel/viele") genannt wird (vgl. Unit 12).**
  He had been looking round the airport shops. He had bought a book and two magazines.

- **Wenn zwei Handlungen hintereinander geschehen und die zweite eine logische Folge oder Reaktion darstellt, werden beide mit der einfachen Vergangenheit ausgedrückt.**
  We left the terminal building and went to the car park.

  Soll aber ausgedrückt werden, dass die erste vorher abgeschlossen wurde, steht diese im Past Perfect.
  I had started the engine when Tom asked if he could drive.

- **In Nebensätzen mit as soon as, after, before, until kann das Past Perfect ODER die Vergangenheit stehen.**
  As soon as / After we (had) left the airport, it started raining. It didn't stop before/until we (had) got home.

Das Wichtigste in Kürze

- Past Perfect, wenn etwas vor einem Zeitpunkt der Vergangenheit abgeschlossen wurde
- Verlaufsform betont Andauern von etwas bis zu einem Zeitpunkt der Vergangenheit
- Keine Verlaufsform bei Zustandsverben und bei Antwort auf Frage „wie viel/viele"

Weitere Informationen → Unit 14

A One sentence has a mistake. Which sentence is correct?

a It had been stopping raining by the evening.
b It had stopped raining by the evening. ✔

1 **a** We got to the cinema late and the film already started.
b We got to the cinema late and the film had already started.

2 **a** When we finally got home, we had been travelling for over 20 hours.
b When we finally got home, we travelled for over 20 hours.

3 **a** Did you go to Australia before your trip last May?
b Had you been to Australia before your trip last May?

4 **a** It was lovely to see Linda last week. I hadn't seen her since we left university.
b It was lovely to see Linda last week. I didn't see her since we left university.

B Make complete sentences using the simple past and the past perfect.

When / we / get to the party / the other guests / already / arrive.
When we got to the party, the other guests had already arrived.

1 I / already / do all the housework / when I / leave home yesterday morning.
2 We / only be abroad once before we / fly to China last year.
3 The little girl / be upset because she / lose her mother in the supermarket.
4 Joe / almost give up / when he finally / find a new job.
5 Our visitors / not arrive on time because their car / break down on the motorway.
6 They / not be married very long when they / decide to get divorced.

C Complete this story using the simple past, the past continuous, the past perfect or the past perfect continuous.

Two years ago Laura .... 1 (have) a very strange Christmas. As usual, she flew home from Germany to spend Christmas with her parents in England. The evening before her flight, she .... 2 (wrap up) all the presents she .... 3 (buy) in the weeks before Christmas. While Laura .... 4 (pack) her suitcase, a friend from England .... 5 (call) and they .... 6 (decide) to meet for coffee at Heathrow Airport as they .... 7 (not see) each other for months.

The next day, Laura .... 8 (wake up) really early feeling very excited. She .... 9 (not be) home since May and .... 10 (look forward to) her holiday with her parents for weeks. The flight .... 11 (land) on time and Laura .... 12 (go) to the baggage reclaim to collect her suitcase. After she .... 13 (wait) for over 20 minutes, she .... 14 (realize) that she was the only person without her luggage. She .... 15 (go) to the airline information desk and .... 16 (fill in) a form with details about her missing suitcase. They .... 17 (tell) her that her suitcase would be delivered the next morning – 24 December.

After Laura .... 18 (meet) her friend for coffee, she .... 19 (take) the bus and train to her parents'. They .... 20 (stand) on the platform when her train .... 21 (arrive) and they .... 22 (be) very surprised when Laura .... 23 (get off) with only her handbag. Laura .... 24 (explain) what .... 25 (happen) while they .... 26 (walk) to the car. The suitcase finally .... 27 (come) on 26 December. The airline .... 28 (send) it to Casablanca by mistake!

14 Overview: Continuous form and simple form
Überblick: Verlaufsform und einfache Form

A: What happened exactly?

B: The other driver just came straight out of a side road, without stopping. I am sure he ~~had drunk~~ had been drinking.

A: Are you OK?

B: Yes, but Tom is suffering from shock. He ~~drove~~ was driving.

A: Can I go in to him?

B: The doctor ~~examines~~ is examining him at the moment.

Verlaufsform – Einfache Form

- **Die Verlaufsform kennzeichnet etwas als im Verlauf begriffen, noch andauernd, nicht abgeschlossen. Die einfache Form kennzeichnet etwas als bestehenden Dauerzustand oder als abgeschlossen.**

What are you doing here? – I'm **waiting** for my son. → I usually **wait** outside. But it's too cold today.
At the time we **were staying** at a hotel in Nice. → We **stayed** there six days, then went to Paris.
I've **been answering** e-mails all morning. → I've **answered** more than 20 so far.
He took a taxi because he **had been drinking**. → He **had drunk** at least half a bottle of wine.

- **Auch mehrere wiederholte Handlungen können mit der Verlaufsform ausgedrückt werden, wenn sie zusammen eine vorübergehende Situation darstellen.**
  Tom **is cycling** to work at the moment. I've **been walking** to work recently. We both want to get fit again.

- **Die Verlaufsform nimmt Bezug auf einen bestimmten Zeitpunkt oder Zeitraum.**

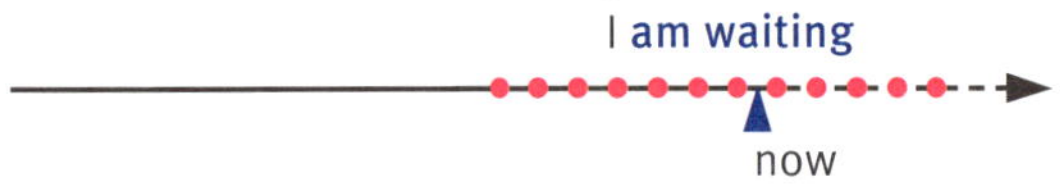

What are you doing here? – I'm **waiting** for Jim.

Gegenwart: jetziger Zeitpunkt. Zum jetzigen Zeitpunkt ist etwas im Verlauf begriffen.

I **was waiting** for Jim when Ann came along.

Vergangenheit: Zeitpunkt der Vergangenheit Zum damaligen Zeitpunkt war etwas im Verlauf begriffen.

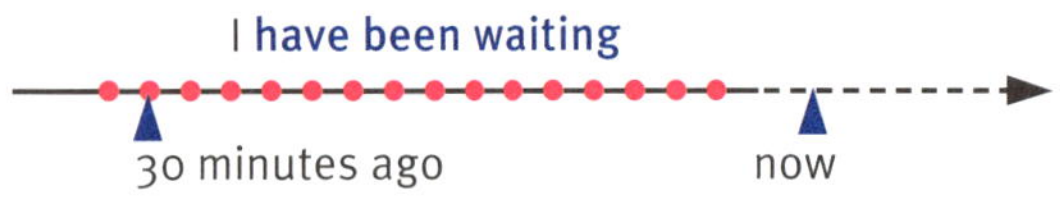

Why are you late? I **have been waiting** for 30 minutes.

Present Perfect: Zeitraum bis (oder fast bis) zum jetzigen Zeitpunkt Bis (oder fast bis) jetzt dauert(e) etwas an.

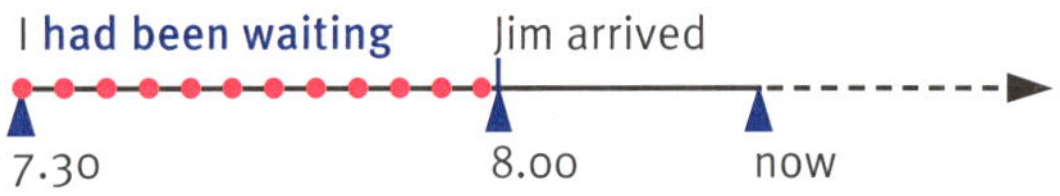

I **had been waiting** for 30 minutes when Jim arrived.

Past Perfect: Zeitraum bis (oder fast bis) zu einem Zeitpunkt der Vergangenheit. Bis (oder fast bis) zum damaligen Zeitpunkt dauerte etwas an.

! **Verben, die Zustände bezeichnen (siehe Liste Unit 4), können in der Regel nicht in der Verlaufsform stehen.**
It's (~~It's being~~) really cold here at the moment. I've known (~~I've been knowing~~) Tom for ages.

Das Wichtigste in Kürze

- **Verlaufsform: im Gange, im Verlauf begriffen, andauernd, nicht abgeschlossen, vorübergehend**
- **einfache Form: jetziger Dauerzustand oder inzwischen/damals abgeschlossen**

Weitere Informationen → Units 2-4, 6, 11-13

A One sentence has a mistake. Which sentence is correct?

a I found this photo when I was looking through some papers. ✓
b I was finding this photo when I looked through some papers.

1 **a** What do you read? It looks interesting.
b What are you reading? It looks interesting.

2 **a** How many English courses have you taken?
b How many English courses have you been taking?

3 **a** Martin didn't seem very happy, did he?
b Martin wasn't seeming very happy, was he?

4 **a** Nobody has been phoning me this week.
b Nobody has phoned me this week.

5 **a** Jo was angry. We had forgotten her birthday.
b Jo was angry. We had been forgetting her birthday.

6 **a** Sorry I'm late. I've been talking to Jim.
b Sorry I'm late. I've talked to Jim.

B Make complete sentences. Use the continuous form where possible.

When we finally arrived, we / drive for over eight hours.
When we finally arrived, we had been driving for over eight hours.

1 I / try to phone Sue all day. Her phone is always engaged.
2 It was great to see Richard last week. We / not / see him since we moved.
3 Bill and Carol had so many arguments when they / travel round Europe that they / decide to come home.
4 My son / work in the local supermarket at the moment – it's a holiday job. He / not / like the work much but he / need the money.
5 When we arrived in Manchester, the sun / shine. Obviously it / rain because the ground was still wet.
6 I / not / look for a new flat for very long before I / find one I liked.

C Complete these dialogues with the verbs in the continuous form where possible.

1 A: Where .... (you/go) when I saw you with Paul on Monday?
I .... (not realize) that you knew each other.
B: We .... (go) to our evening class. We are both learning Spanish.
2 A: How .... (Tom/break) his leg?
B: He .... (fall) off the ladder when he .... (clean) the windows. He was in a hurry because the football match .... (already start) and he wanted to watch it.
3 A: When our friends .... (stay) with us, we decided to go for a long walk on Saturday. We .... (only walk) for ten minutes when it started to rain.
B: I know, the weather was terrible, wasn't it? I had just finished cleaning the car when it .... (start) to rain.
4 A: We haven't had a holiday this year. We were planning to go to Canada and America, but then my wife .... (lose) her job at the paint factory at the beginning of the year, so we .... (decide) we couldn't afford to go away.
B: We haven't been away this year, either. We .... (save) for the last few months – we want to buy a bigger house.
5 A: Sorry, I .... (not listen). What did you say? Are we meeting the others outside the restaurant or inside?
B: Inside, and we're late. They .... (probably wait) for ages. I hope they .... (order) a drink.

D Translate the following sentences. Use the continuous form where possible.

1 Paul lernt Spanisch. Er lernt es seit zwei Monaten. Der Kurs findet montags statt. (stattfinden = *take place*)
2 Hast du gehört? Tom hat sich das Bein gebrochen. Es ist letzte Woche passiert, als er die Fenster putzte.
3 Ich hatte auf eine Gelegenheit (*opportunity*) gewartet, das Auto zu waschen. Ich trocknete es gerade, als ich die schwarzen Wolken sah.
4 Meine Frau sucht seit Anfang des Jahres eine neue Stelle. Als sie ihre Stelle verlor, hatte sie schon über 20 Jahre bei der Firma gearbeitet.
5 Wir sind gestern zu spät gekommen. Unsere Freunde warteten schon seit einer halben Stunde, als wir endlich ankamen.

15 Future (1): will
Zukunft (1): will

A: This menu is so big. It's difficult to decide what to eat.
B: I ~~will~~ want something with fish.
A: Hmm. They've got scampi, look here, with chips and salad.
B: Oh yes, I hadn't seen that. ~~I take~~ I'll take that.
A: And for me, I think, lasagne. OK. Now, where's that waiter?
B: He ~~is~~ will be here in a minute.

Form

- will: Kurzform 'll, Verneinung won't

You'll see Tom at the party next week, but Ann won't be there.
Will Sonia be there? – Yes, she will. / No, she won't.

! Englisch will – Deutsch „will/wollen"

Deutsch „will/wollen" zum Ausdruck eines Wunsches entspricht want to, nicht ~~will~~.

Tanja will einen Hund. Sie will einen Pudel kaufen. Tanja wants (~~will~~) a dog. She wants to buy a poodle.

! Englisch will – Deutsch Gegenwart

Im Deutschen steht oft die Gegenwart, wo im Englischen will/won't stehen muss.

Ich sehe dich morgen. I'll see (~~I see~~) you tomorrow.

Vorhersagen

- Mit will und won't macht man Vorhersagen über Dinge, die sicher und nicht beeinflussbar sind.
  We will know (~~We know~~) the result tomorrow. It will be (~~It is~~) in all the papers.
  We have to put the clocks back an hour tonight. It'll be (~~It is~~) dark at this time tomorrow.
- Die Vorhersage beruht oft auf Erfahrungswerten. Man kann sie mit perhaps, probably usw. einschränken.
  It's Sunday so we (probably) won't have (~~don't have~~) any problems finding somewhere to park.
- will steht oft nach I think, I expect, I hope, I'm certain/sure/afraid.
  I expect I'll see (~~I see~~) Christine at the party this evening.

Spontane Entschlüsse

- will/won't wird gebraucht, um spontane Entschlüsse (oft z.B. Angebote) auszudrücken.
  Oh, the phone's ringing. – I'll answer (~~I answer~~) it.
  Red wine or white? – I won't (~~don't~~) have any wine, thanks. I'll just have (~~I just have~~) water.
  I'll carry (~~I carry~~) that suitcase for you.

Bereitschaft

- Mit will/won't drückt man (Nicht-)Bereitschaft aus (auch z.B. als Versprechen/Drohung).
  Tom will take (~~takes~~) us to the airport, I'm sure. Let's ask him.
  They want to cut down these trees, but I won't (~~don't~~) let them do it.
  I'll be (~~I am~~) there, I promise.
  I'll throw (~~I throw~~) you out if you say another word.

Das Wichtigste in Kürze

- Deutsch „will/wollen" = want to; Englisch will entspricht „werden"
- Mit will drückt man aus: Vorhersagen; spontane Entschlüsse, z.B. Angebote; Bereitschaft

Weitere Informationen → Units 16-17

A One sentence has a mistake. Which sentence is correct?

a My son will study in the USA.
b My son wants to study in the USA. ✔

1 **a** Can I speak to Tom, please? – Yes, I get him.
b Can I speak to Tom, please? – Yes, I'll get him.

2 **a** Jamie wants a bicycle for Christmas.
b Jamie will a bicycle for Christmas.

3 **a** I don't help you if you don't switch the TV off.
b I won't help you if you don't switch the TV off.

4 **a** I don't want to move but my wife has a new job.
b I will not move but my wife has a new job.

5 **a** That bag is too heavy for you. I carry it.
b That bag is too heavy for you. I'll carry it.

6 **a** Cheese or ham sandwich? – I'll have ham, please.
b Cheese or ham sandwich? – I have ham, please.

B Make complete sentences using the will future.

I'm busy. I / help you later. *I'm busy. I'll help you later.*

1 Jo's invited us to her party next week. She / be 18.
2 My mother / probably / come for Christmas.
3 If you take this bag, I / carry the heavy suitcase.
4 The weather forecast says it / rain tomorrow.
5 The roads are so busy. I hope we / not be late.
6 I / post your letter for you if you like.

C Complete these dialogues with want to or the will future.

A: I *want to* make a cake as Sue is coming round tomorrow. Did you remember to buy some eggs?
B: Sorry I forgot. I*'ll* go shopping later.

1 A: Paul phoned an hour ago. They .... come this weekend.
B: Great! I .... try to get some theatre tickets.

2 A: I'm sorry. Gary's gone out. I .... tell him you called.
B: Thanks. I .... try again later.

3 A: I've got such a bad headache. I think I .... call my Spanish teacher to say I probably .... (not) be there this evening.
B: I .... get you an aspirin – perhaps if you lie down for an hour, you .... feel better.

4 A: I .... have a party for my birthday but I .... (not) make all the food myself. I think I .... order the food from a party service.
B: That .... be expensive. I .... make the desserts if you like.

5 A: We've put our house on the market. We .... buy a bigger one. Jack's mother .... be eighty next month and we think it would be better if she lived with us.
B: Do you really think she .... agree to move at her age?

D Translate the following sentences. Where possible, use will.

1 Hast du einen Regenschirm? Ich bin sicher, dass du später einen brauchst.
2 Jill will mehr Geld. Ich denke, sie sieht sich bald nach einer neuen Stelle um. (sich umsehen = *look for*)
3 Vergiss nicht, Briefmarken zu kaufen. – Nein, ich vergesse es nicht!
4 Welchen Film wollt ihr euch anschauen?
5 Ich helfe dir später. Heute Nachmittag will ich ein Geburtstagsgeschenk für meine Tante kaufen. Wenn ich zurück bin, rufe ich dich an.

16 Future (2): going to, present continuous, simple present
Zukunft (2): going to, Verlaufsform, einfache Form der Gegenwart

A: What are your holiday plans? Do you know yet?
B: Oh, yes. We ~~will visit~~ *are going to visit / are visiting* some friends in France.
A: That's nice. So you plan to take the car, I suppose.
B: No, we ~~fly.~~ *are going to fly / are flying* They have two cars, so we won't need ours. Oh, look at those black clouds.
A: Perhaps we should go inside.
B: Yes. ~~It rains~~ *It's going to rain* in a minute.

going to

- **Mit going to sagt man, was auf Grund bestehender Vorzeichen geschehen wird.**
  Look at all this traffic. We're going to be late. *Sieh dir diesen Verkehr an. Wir werden uns verspäten.*
  Careful! You're going to knock my glass over! *Vorsicht! Du wirfst mein Glas gleich um.*
- **going to wird ferner gebraucht, um vorüberlegte Entschlüsse und Pläne auszudrücken.**
  We're going to buy a new car. We've already sold our old one.
  Jane isn't going to stay on at school after July. She's going to look for a job.

  Vergleiche:
  I'm going to park in the station car park. There's never a space in this road. [= vorüberlegter Entschluss]
  Ich parke auf dem Bahnhofsparkplatz. In dieser Straße findet man nie eine Parklücke.
  Oh, look. There is a space today. OK, I'll park here. [= spontaner Entschluss]
  Ach, schau. Heute gibt es eine Lücke. Gut, ich parke hier.

Verlaufsform der Gegenwart

- **Die Verlaufsform der Gegenwart verwendet man, wenn für etwas Zukünftiges bereits Vorkehrungen oder Abmachungen getroffen sind, oder wenn man für sich eine bestimmte Zeiteinteilung vorgenommen hat.**
  I'm meeting Ann for a meal tomorrow evening. I've booked a table for 7.30 at the Italian restaurant.
  I've got a busy week. Tomorrow I'm painting the kitchen, and on Friday I'm doing the bathroom.

  Wenn sich die Verlaufsform auf die Zukunft bezieht, wird sie meist mit einer Zeitbestimmung gebraucht, z.B. next week, on Friday, at seven o'clock usw.
- **Oft kann die Verlaufsform oder going to ohne wesentlichen Bedeutungsunterschied gebraucht werden.**
  Next Sunday I'm meeting Phil [= ist ausgemacht] / I'm going to meet Phil [= vorüberlegter Plan].

Einfache Form der Gegenwart

- **Die einfache Form der Gegenwart verwendet man, wenn etwas durch einen Fahrplan, ein Programm usw. vorgegeben ist.**
  My train arrives at 7.43 and the concert starts at 8.

Das Wichtigste in Kürze

- going to = etwas steht (unmittelbar) bevor: „Ich sehe es schon kommen"
- going to = Plan oder Absicht: „Das habe ich fest vor"
- Verlaufsform der Gegenwart + Zeitbestimmung = vorbereiteter Plan: „Dafür habe ich Vorkehrungen/Abmachungen getroffen"
- einfache Gegenwart = „Fahrplan-Zukunft": „Das ist durch Fahrplan/Programm vorgegeben"

A One sentence has a mistake. Which sentence is correct?

a It's Ann's birthday tomorrow. I make a cake.
b It's Ann's birthday tomorrow. I'm going to make a cake. ✔

1 **a** Is the film starting at 7.30 or 8 o'clock?
b Does the film start at 7.30 or 8 o'clock?

2 **a** What do you do this weekend?
b What are you doing this weekend?

3 **a** Are you seeing your family this Christmas?
b Do you see your family this Christmas?

4 **a** Hurry up! We're going to miss the bus.
b Hurry up! We're missing the bus.

5 **a** The wind blows that tree down soon.
b The wind is going to blow that tree down soon.

6 **a** We don't have a holiday this year.
b We aren't going to have a holiday this year.

B Make complete sentences or questions using the present continuous or the simple present.

I / visit my relatives in Australia next month. *I'm visiting my relatives in Australia next month.*

1 I / meet / a friend after work tomorrow. ....

2 Jane's train / arrive at 11.30 or 12.30? ....

3 We / not have a holiday this summer. We / stay here. ....

4 Here is a list of the people we / invite to our wedding. ....

5 The concert / start / at 8 o'clock. ....

6 What / you do this evening? ....

C Complete these dialogues using going to or the will future.

A: I*'m going to get* **(get)** Ann a CD for her birthday. What about you?
B: I've no idea. I think I*'ll ask* **(ask)** her what she would like.

1 A: Has your son decided what he wants to do when he leaves school?
B: Yes. He .... **(not apply)** for a place at university.
He .... **(travel)** round the world for a year!

2 A: I .... **(give)** you and Sue a lift to the airport if you like.
B: Yes, please! I .... **(ring)** Sue and tell her.

3 A: Look at the time. We .... **(be)** late.
B: I hope they .... **(not think)** that we're not coming.

4 A: Dave .... **(buy)** tickets for the big football match next month. Do you want one?
B: No, thanks. I'm sure they .... **(show)** it on TV.

5 A: Do you know anyone who wants a winter coat? I .... **(throw)** this one away.
B: Don't do that. I .... **(take)** it to the Red Cross.

D Translate the following sentences.

1 Sei vorsichtig! Die Vase fällt [gleich] um (*over*).
2 Ich fahre euch, wenn ihr wollt. – Danke, aber es ist alles organisiert. Wir nehmen ein Taxi.
3 Wann fängt der Film an?
4 Unser Chef heiratet nächste Woche. Wir kaufen ihm eine Schürze (*apron*) als Hochzeitsgeschenk.
5 Ich gehe spazieren. – Gute Idee. Ich komme mit.

17 Future (3): future continuous, future perfect
Zukunft (3): will + Verlaufsform, vollendete Zukunft

A: I hate Mondays, but this time next week ~~I'm lying~~ I will be lying on a beach in Portugal.
B: Lucky you!
A: The flight is on Saturday, so by Monday I ~~will already spend~~ will already have spent one long, lazy day in the sun.
B: Don't forget that you have to come back, though!
A: After four weeks I ~~won't be knowing~~ won't know what this place looks like.
B: You soon will!

Form

■ **will** + Verlaufsform: **will** + **be ...ing**	Next week I**'ll be enjoying** myself. I **won't be sitting** in the office. **Will** you **be travelling** a lot? – Yes, I **will**. / No, I **won't**.
■ Vollendete Zukunft: **will** + **have** + Partizip Perfekt	By (*Bis*) Friday I **will have finished** my exams. I **won't have heard** the results. **Will** you **have had** a party? – Yes, I **will**. / No, I **won't**.

will + Verlaufsform

■ **will** + Verlaufsform drückt aus, dass eine Handlung oder vorübergehende Situation zu einem zukünftigen Zeitpunkt im Verlauf begriffen, nicht abgeschlossen sein wird, d.h. noch andauern wird.

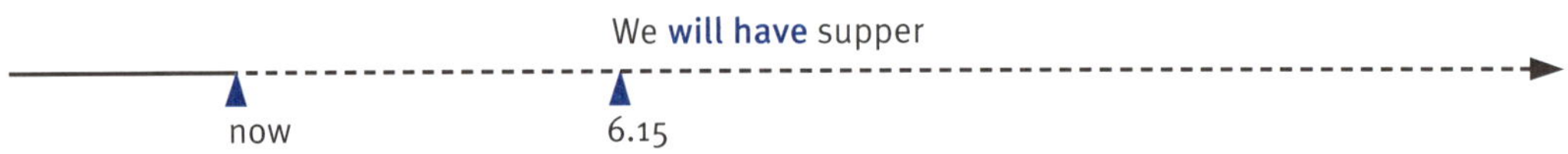

At 6.15 we will have supper. [= Um 18.15 werden wir anfangen zu essen.]

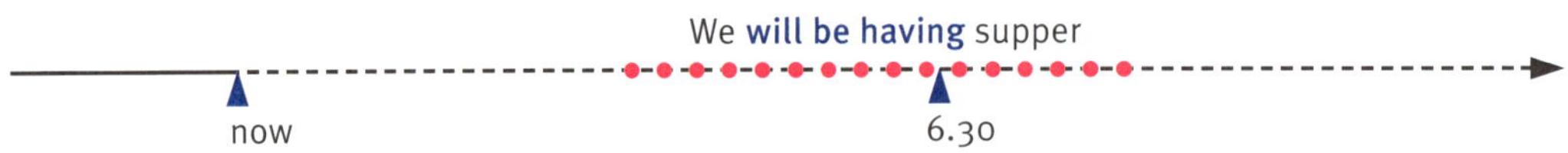

At 6.30 we will be having supper. [= Um 18.30 werden wir gerade beim Essen sein.]

Don't phone at 6.30. We**'ll** still **be having** supper. ... *Wir werden noch beim Abendessen sein.*
If you phone later, my dad **will** probably **be watching** TV. ..., *wird mein Papa ... beim Fernsehen sein.*

! Die Verlaufsform kann nicht mit Zustandsverben gebraucht werden (siehe Liste Unit 4).
It **will seem** (~~will be seeming~~) strange to go away without the children.

Vollendete Zukunft

■ Mit der vollendeten Zukunft wird ausgedrückt, was bis zu einem bestimmten zukünftigen Zeitpunkt abgeschlossen sein wird. Häufiges Signalwort: **by** (*bis*).
We can phone them now, I think. They **will have got up** now.
Wir können sie jetzt anrufen. Jetzt werden sie aufgestanden sein.
By the end of the holiday we**'ll** probably **have driven** more than 5000 kilometres.
Bis zum Ende des Urlaubs werden wir wahrscheinlich mehr als 5000 Kilometer gefahren sein.

Das Wichtigste in Kürze

- **will be ...ing**: etwas wird zu einem zukünftigen Zeitpunkt im Gange sein
- **will have ...ed**: etwas wird zu einem zukünftigen Zeitpunkt fertig abgeschlossen sein

A One sentence has a mistake. Which sentence is correct?

a If you need to phone me next week, I'll be staying at the George Hotel. ✔
b If you need to phone me next week, I'll stay at the George Hotel.

1 **a** We're late. The film will have already started by the time we get there.
b We're late. The film will already start by the time we get there.

2 **a** Don't call them now. They'll be having lunch.
b Don't call them now. They'll have lunch.

3 **a** Next month we'll have known each other for twenty years.
b Next month we'll be knowing each other for twenty years.

4 **a** By Easter we will save enough for a trip to Canada.
b By Easter we will have saved enough for a trip to Canada.

B Make complete sentences using the future continuous and the future perfect.

(I always leave home at 8 o'clock and get to work at 8.45.)
By 8.15 / I / leave home — By 8.15 I will have left home.
By 9.00 / I / arrive at work — By 9.00 I will have arrived at work.
At 9.10 / I / work — At 9.10 I will be working.

1 (We have Sunday lunch at 1 o'clock. Sam cooks it and I do the washing up. I usually finish by 2.30.)
At 12 o'clock / Sam / cook / lunch ....
At 1.10 / we / eat ....
At 2.45 / I / do the washing up ....

2 (The children leave home at 8.15 and take the bus to school. The first lesson is from 9.00 to 9.45 and the second is from 9.45 to 10.30.)
At 8.30 / they / travel to school ....
At 9.30 / they / sit in their first lesson ....
By 10.40 / they / have two lessons ....

3 (It's 11.00 on Monday. My cleaning woman comes on Tuesdays and works from 10.00–1.00, then she goes to my neighbour's.)
This time tomorrow my cleaning woman / start work ....
By 1.30 she / finish work in my flat ....
At 1.30 she / clean my neighbour's flat ....

C Complete these dialogues with the future continuous and the future perfect. If they are not possible, use will.

1 A: Do you think Sue and Frank .... **(arrive)** by the time I get home from work?
B: I don't know. I .... **(phone)** them and ask when they hope to leave.

2 A: I'm sure England .... **(win)** the match tomorrow.
B: It doesn't really worry me. This time tomorrow I .... **(sit)** in the plane on my way to New York.

3 A: I think I .... **(ring)** Terry and Diane before we go out.
B: Don't ring them now. They .... **(eat)** dinner.

4 A: I .... **(help)** you decorate your kitchen when I get back from holiday.
B: Thanks, but I hope we .... **(finish)** by the time you get back.

D Translate the following sentences.

1 Nächstes Jahr sind meine Eltern schon 40 Jahre verheiratet.
2 Morgen um diese Zeit liege ich am Strand.
3 Ellen wird schon angekommen sein. Es ist schon nach 11.00.
4 Bis Dienstag werde ich dieses Buch gelesen haben. Dann kannst du es haben.
5 Ich rufe morgen an. – OK, aber nicht zwischen 19.00 und 20.00 Uhr, weil wir gerade beim Essen sein werden.

18 Questions (1): Yes/No questions and short answers
Fragen (1): Entscheidungsfragen und Kurzantworten

A: ~~Play you~~ Do you play poker?
B: No, I'm afraid not. I don't really play many card games.
A: ~~Do you~~ Do you do any sport?
B: Yes, I do. I play squash in the winter and tennis in the summer. Do you like tennis?
A: Yes, ~~I like~~ I do. I'm a member of the Grün-Weiß club.
B: How about a game one day? I hope you're not too good!

Fragebildung mit und ohne do

- Wenn ein Aussagesatz ein Hilfsverb enthält, bildet man die dazugehörige Frage (wie im Deutschen) durch Umstellung von Subjekt und Verb.
  Steht ein Vollverb (außer be) im Aussagesatz, muss eine Form von do (do, does oder did) als Hilfsverb eingesetzt werden.

– Hilfsverben zur Zeitenbildung: be, have, will Frage: Hilfsverb + Subjekt + Vollverb	Tom is coming. Tom was running. Tom has left. Tom will be late.	Is Ann coming? Was Ann running? Has Ann left? Will Ann be late?
– Modale Hilfsverben: can, should, may, might usw. Frage: Hilfsverb + Subjekt + Vollverb	Tom can come. Tom should wait.	Can Ann come? Should Ann wait?
– be als Vollverb: Frage: Form von be + Subjekt	Tom is English.	Is Ann English?
– Vollverben außer be Frage: Hilfsverb do/does/did + Subjekt + Vollverb	Tom plays tennis. Tom phoned.	Does Ann play tennis? Did Ann phone?

- Fragen mit dem Vollverb have werden mit do/does/did gebildet, Fragen mit have got jedoch ohne.
  Tom has time. — Does Ann have time?
  Tom has got time. — Has Ann got time?

Kurzantworten

- Ein schlichtes Yes oder No als Antwort wird oft als unhöflich empfunden, deshalb empfiehlt es sich, stets die volle Kurzantwort zu verwenden. Dabei wird das Hilfsverb der Frage wieder aufgegriffen.
  Is David coming? – Yes, he is. / No, he isn't.
  Was Ann waiting? – Yes, she was. / No, she wasn't.
  Has my letter arrived? – Yes, it has. / No, it hasn't.
  Will it be cold? – Yes, it will. / No, it won't.
  Can you see? – Yes, I can. / No, I can't.
  Do you smoke? – Yes, I do. / No, I don't.
  Does Janet know? – Yes, she does. / No, she doesn't.
  Did it rain? – Yes, it did. / No, it didn't.
- Auch bei Fragen mit dem Vollverb be und have got wird das Verb der Frage wiederholt.
  Is Tony here?– Yes, he is. / No, he isn't.
  Have you got time?– Yes, I have. / No, I haven't.

Das Wichtigste in Kürze

- Fragen mit einem Vollverb: Form von do verwenden
- Volle Kurzantworten sind höflicher – Hilfsverb der Frage wiederholen

Weitere Informationen → Units 19-20

A One sentence has a mistake. Which sentence is correct?

a Lives David in London?
b Does David live in London? ✔

1 **a** Do you know what time the film starts?
b Know you what time the film starts?

2 **a** Have you seen my keys anywhere?
b You have seen my keys anywhere?

3 **a** Can you play chess? – Yes, I play.
b Can you play chess? – Yes, I can.

4 **a** Does your son have got his own car?
b Has your son got his own car?

5 **a** Was it snowing when you left? – Yes, it did.
b Was it snowing when you left? – Yes, it was.

6 **a** What does your husband do? – He's a doctor.
b What does your husband? – He's a doctor.

B Give short answers for the following questions.

A: Can you play the piano? B: No, *I can't*.

1 A: Do you like your new job? B: Yes, ...

2 A: Are your parents coming for Christmas? B: Yes, ...

3 A: Did Paul phone yesterday? B: No, ...

4 A: Have the children tidied their rooms? B: Yes, ...

5 A: Does Sue still live in Manchester? B: No, ...

C Make questions and short answers. Be careful with the different tenses!

you / have time to help me now? – Yes.
Do you have time to help me now? – Yes, I do.

your husband / go to Leeds last week? – No, he / not.
Did your husband go to Leeds last week? – No, he didn't.

1 you / know where the post office is, please? – No, I'm sorry, I / not.

....

2 the children / do their homework yet? – Yes.

....

3 you / go shopping yesterday? – Yes.

....

4 Sally / come tomorrow? – No, I'm afraid she / not.

....

5 Paul / ever be abroad? – No, he / not.

....

D Translate the following questions and short answers.

1 Hast du meine Autoschlüssel gesehen? – Nein.
2 Warst du gestern in der Schule? – Ja.
3 Geht ihr heute Abend ins Kino? – Ja.
4 Kann Tom schwimmen? – Nein.
5 Hast du Janes neue Adresse? – Ja.

19 Questions (2): wh-questions with/without do, with preposition
Fragen (1): wh-Fragen mit/ohne „do“, mit Präposition

A: Who ~~did phone~~ *phoned* so late last night?
B: It was Julia, a colleague from work.
A: What ~~wanted she~~ *did she want*?
B: She hasn't got a car today. She asked if she can come with me.
A: ~~With who works she?~~ *Who does she work with?* Is she in your team?
B: No, she's in export.

wh-Fragen mit und ohne do bei Vollverben

- Fragen mit when, where, how und why werden mit einer Form von do gebildet.

	Tom	teaches	English	at the Volkshochschule	on Wednesday evening.
When does	Tom	teach	English	at the Volkshochschule?	
Where does	Tom	teach	English		on Wednesday evening?

- who-Fragen werden ohne do gebildet, wenn who dem deutschen „wer“ entspricht.
  who-Fragen werden mit do gebildet, wenn who dem deutschen „wen“ (oder „wem“) entspricht.

	Tom	teaches	**Anja**.		
	Who	teaches	**Anja**?	– Tom. He's the teacher.	*Wer unterrichtet Anja?*
Who does	*Tom*	teach?		– Anja. She's a student.	*Wen unterrichtet Tom?*

who = „wer“ bezeichnet das Subjekt des Satzes – die Person, die etwas tut.
who = „wen“ bezeichnet das Objekt des Satzes – die Person, der etwas getan wird.

- Fragen mit what, which und how much/many werden ohne do gebildet, wenn das Fragewort Subjekt (oder Teil des Subjekts) ist, dagegen mit do, wenn das Fragewort Objekt (oder Teil des Objekts) ist.

Tom watched some videos with his students last week.

***What* happened** last week?	*Was ist letzte Woche passiert?*
What **did *Tom* do** last week?	*Was hat Tom letzte Woche getan?*
Which video **interested** the class most?	*Welches Video interessierte die Klasse am meisten?*
Which videos **did *the class* watch**?	*Welche Videos hat die Klasse angeschaut?*
How many students **watched**?	*Wie viele Kursteilnehmer/innen haben zugeschaut?*
How many videos **did *they* watch**?	*Wie viele Videos haben sie angeschaut?*

Fragen mit Präpositionen

- In diesen Fragen entspricht who ... with? dem deutschen „mit wem“, who ... to? dem deutschen „wem“.

Anja went sailing with Tom last week.
Who did Anja go sailing with ?
Mit wem ist Anja segeln gegangen?

She introduced him to her friends.
Who did she introduce him to ?
Wem hat sie ihn vorgestellt?

Die Präposition (hier: with, to) steht normalerweise dort, wo sie auch sonst steht: hinter dem Verb und ggf. dessen Objekt – nicht, wie im Deutschen, vor dem Fragewort.

- Diese Stellung der Präposition gilt auch in anderen Fragen.

He is looking for a present for a friend.
What is he looking for ?

Her friend comes from Colombia.
Where does her friend come from ?

Das Wichtigste in Kürze

- who? = „wen?/wem?“: Frage mit do bilden
- Präpositionen stehen in Fragen am Ende, nicht vor dem Fragewort

Weitere Informationen → Unit 20

A One sentence has a mistake. Which sentence is correct?

a Why did you phone Jill yesterday? ✔
b Why phoned you Jill yesterday?

1 **a** What kind of holidays do you prefer?
b What kind of holidays prefer you?

2 **a** With who did you go to the cinema?
b Who did you go to the cinema with?

3 **a** How did Tom break his leg? What did happen?
b How did Tom break his leg? What happened?

4 **a** Who answered the phone when you called Steve?
b Who did answer the phone when you called Steve?

5 **a** Who looked after the children while you were away?
b Who did look after the children while you were away?

6 **a** How many people went to Jane's party?
b How many people did go to Jane's party?

B Make questions for these answers.

When / happen / the accident? – It happened last week.
When did the accident happen?

1 Who / Jane / share a flat / with? – She lives with two friends.

2 How many people / come to your birthday party last week? – Over thirty.

3 What wine / go / best with beef: red or white? – Red wine, I think.

4 Who / help you / with your homework? – Nobody, I did it myself!

5 What / normally happen / at Christmas in your office? – We usually all go out for dinner.

C Make questions for these answers.

A: What *did you do yesterday evening*?
B: I went to the opera.

1 A: Who ....?

B: I went with a colleague.

2 A: Who ....?

B: My colleague paid for the tickets.

3 A: What .... after the opera?

B: We met some friends at the theatre, so we all went for a drink.

4 A: How many of you .... altogether?

B: There were six of us.

5 A: Who .... in the pub?

B: I sat next to Paul.

6 A: What ....?

B: We talked about his new flat.

D Translate the following questions.

1 Was ist letzte Woche passiert? Wie ist der Unfall passiert?
2 Wer hat gestern so spät angerufen?
3 Mit wem bist du gestern einkaufen gegangen?
4 Wer hat dir diese Postkarte geschickt?
5 Wem hast du geschrieben, als du im Urlaub warst?

20 Questions (3): Question tags
Fragen (3): Frageanhängsel

A: I expect you're ready for a cup of coffee, ~~no?~~ aren't you?
B: Yes, please. That would be lovely.

A: You take sugar, ~~yes?~~ don't you?
B: Yes, please. Three spoonfuls.

A: Three! Your dentist will get rich from you, ~~will she?~~ won't she?
B: She's rich enough already. I just like it sweet.

Form

- **Frageanhängsel (oder „Bestätigungsfragen") entsprechen „nicht wahr?" bzw. „oder?" im Deutschen. Sie werden durch Wiederholung eines Hilfsverbs gebildet.**

  You**'re** learning Spanish, **aren't** you?
  Ann **has** been to Ireland, **hasn't** she?
  It **won't** be cold there in May, **will** it?
  She **must** be Italian, **mustn't** she?
  Tom **can't** speak Chinese, **can** he?

  Ein bejahtes Hilfsverb (z.B. has) wird verneint ans Satzende gestellt (hasn't).
  Ein verneintes Hilfsverb (z.B. can't) wird bejaht ans Satzende gestellt (can).

- **Wie in anderen Fragen muss man eine Form von do einsetzen, wenn sonst kein Hilfsverb vorhanden ist.**

  You **read** a lot, **don't** you?
  You **don't watch** much TV, **do** you?
  Tom **plays** tennis, **doesn't** he?
  He **doesn't play** hockey, **does** he?
  They **flew**, **didn't** they?
  They **didn't go** by car, **did** they?

- **Beachten Sie zwei Ausnahmen.**

1. **I am** late, **aren't I** (~~amn't I~~)?
   I am getting better, **aren't I** (~~amn't I~~)?
2. **Let's** (= Let us) go, **shall we**?

Intonation und Gebrauch

You still love me, **don't you?** ↗
I've only got $20. It won't cost too much, **will it?** ↗
Tom doesn't really speak Arabic, **does he?** ↗

Geht die Stimme am Satzende hoch, bedeutet dies: „Ich bin mir nicht sicher. Sage mir, ob es wahr ist." Manchmal wird damit Überraschung ausgedrückt: „Das überrascht mich. Ist es wirklich wahr?"

Ann drives a VW, **doesn't she?** ↘ She's got a Golf.
You don't need me, **do you?** ↘ I can see that you have lots of help already.

Geht die Stimme nach unten, bedeutet dies: „Ich weiß es eigentlich. Bestätige mir, dass ich recht habe."

Das Wichtigste in Kürze

- **Frageanhängsel sind spiegelbildlich: bejahter Satz – verneintes Anhängsel (und umgekehrt)**
- **Hilfsverb im Satz vorhanden: Hilfsverb im Anhängsel wiederholen**
- **Kein Hilfsverb im Satz vorhanden: Frageanhängsel mit einer Form von do**

A One sentence has a mistake. Which sentence is correct?

a You weren't at work yesterday, were you? ✔
b You weren't at work yesterday, was you?

1 **a** You won't be late, will you?
b You won't be late, won't you?

2 **a** You don't mind if I don't come, do you?
b You don't mind if I don't come, don't you?

3 **a** I'm wrong, am not I?
b I'm wrong, aren't I?

4 **a** They haven't got time, have they?
b They don't have time, have they?

5 **a** He's been very busy lately, isn't he?
b He's been very busy lately, hasn't he?

6 **a** I'm not going to pass the exam, am I?
b I'm not going to pass the exam, are I?

B Add question tags to these questions.

You weren't angry with me, *were you*?

1 I've told you about my holiday, ...?
2 It's much warmer today, ...?
3 You don't really expect him to phone, ...?
4 You live next door to Bill, ...?
5 Your son went to school with Jenny, ...?
6 I'm asking too many questions, ...?

C Make questions with question tags for these answers.

A: You *didn't stay at home* yesterday, *did you*?
B: No, of course I didn't stay at home. I went to Jane's party.

1 A: You .... with me, ...?
B: No, I'm not angry. I just wish you had told me sooner.

2 A: Jackie .... a new job, ...?
B: Yes, she has. She found it through a friend.

3 A: The children .... in the garden, ...?
B: Yes, they are. Look – they're playing behind the trees.

4 A: You .... upset if I don't come to your wedding, ...?
B: No, of course I won't. I understand that it's a long way for you to come.

5 A: You .... lend me ten euros, ...?
B: Well, I could. But what about the ten euros I lent you last week?

6 A: Paul .... next week, ...?
B: Yes, that's right. He's moving on Thursday.

D Translate the following questions.

1 Du kommst morgen, oder?
2 Das war sehr teuer, nicht wahr?
3 John hat gestern nicht angerufen, oder?
4 Ihr wohnt noch nicht lange hier, oder?
5 Das Buch ist sehr interessant, nicht wahr?

The passive (1)
Das Passiv (1)

A: These photos are of Morely Road, aren't they? When ~~are~~ were they taken?
B: Oh, a long time ago. Fifteen or twenty years ago.

A: A lot of new buildings ~~are built~~ have been built since then.
B: Yes, the Barton Hotel, for example.

A: That was opened ~~from~~ by a TV star. Do you remember?
B: Oh yes, that's right. Someone from that Saturday soap opera, wasn't it?

Form

- **Das Passiv wird mit einer Form von be + Partizip Perfekt gebildet.**

Einfache Gegenwart	English **is spoken** all over the world. *Englisch wird ... gesprochen.*
Einfache Vergangenheit	The letter **was posted** in Hamburg. *Der Brief wurde ... abgeschickt.*
Present Perfect	How many copies **have been made**? *Wie viele Kopien sind gemacht worden?*
Past Perfect	The Mercedes **had been stolen** earlier. *Der Mercedes war ... gestohlen worden.*
will-Zukunft	Your questions **will be answered** later. *Ihre Fragen werden ... beantwortet werden.*

- **be answered im letzten Beispielsatz ist die Infinitivform des Passivs. Sie wird auch nach Modalverben wie can, must, may, might, should usw. gebraucht.**
  All bags **must be checked**. *... müssen kontrolliert werden.*
  Messages **can be left** at reception. *... können ... hinterlassen werden.*

Gebrauch

- **In einem Aktivsatz wird gesagt, was jemand (oder etwas) aktiv tut. In einem Passivsatz wird gesagt, was mit jemandem (oder etwas) getan wird.**

Aktivsatz	Some hooligans **attacked** me. *Ein paar Hooligans haben mich überfallen.*
Passivsatz	I **was attacked** from behind. *Ich wurde von hinten überfallen.*

- **In einem Passivsatz kann die Person, die aktiv etwas tut, mit by genannt werden.**
  I **was attacked by** (~~from~~) hooligans. *Ich wurde von Hooligans überfallen.*

  Die meisten Passivsätze haben jedoch keine by-Fügung, denn sehr oft wird das Passiv gebraucht, weil es unwichtig, unbekannt oder auch offensichtlich ist, wer aktiv handelt.
  The road **has been closed**. [Wichtig ist nur, dass die Straße geschlossen ist – von wem, ist unwichtig.]
  Oh look, a window **has been broken**. [Wer das Fenster kaputtgemacht hat, ist unbekannt.]
  The man **was arrested**. [Wer die Verhaftung vorgenommen hat – die Polizei – ist offensichtlich und braucht nicht extra erwähnt zu werden.]

- **Englische Passivsätze entsprechen oft deutschen Sätzen mit „man" .**
  Squash **is played** indoors. *Squash spielt man drinnen.*
  Telegrams **are delivered** straightaway. *Telegramme liefert man sofort aus.*
  I **was told** Tom is coming. *Man hat mir gesagt, Tom kommt.*

Das Wichtigste in Kürze

- **Passivbildung: be + Partizip Perfekt (z.B. is eaten, was made)**
- **„von/durch" = by, nicht ~~from~~: He was met by his wife =** *Er wurde von seiner Frau abgeholt*
- **Sätze mit „man": oft Passivsatz im Englischen**

Weitere Informationen → Unit 22

A One sentence has a mistake. Which sentence is correct?

a This book is written by Charles Dickens.
b This book was written by Charles Dickens. ✔

1 **a** Orders can made by phone.
b Orders can be made by phone.

2 **a** Talks will hold in Washington next week.
b Talks will be held in Washington next week.

3 **a** Have you got any books by Hemingway?
b Have you got any books from Hemingway?

4 **a** The castle is built in the eighteenth century.
b The castle was built in the eighteenth century.

5 **a** The front door should locked in the evening.
b The front door should be locked in the evening.

6 **a** My bicycle has been stolen.
b My bicycle is stolen.

B Make passive sentences.

This church / build / in 1886. *This church was built in 1886.*

1 The Sydney Opera House / design / a Danish architect. ....

2 The new art gallery / open / next week / the Queen. ....

3 'Travelled' / spell / with one 'l' in American English. ....

4 Bags / must not / take / into the museum. ....

5 A lot of people / kill / in road accidents so far this year. ....

C Make questions for these answers.

A: When / the church / build? *When was the church built?*
B: In 1682.

1 A: What / make / in this factory? ....
B: Electronic goods.

2 A: When / new airport / build? ....
B: Next year, I think.

3 A: How long ago / new concert hall / open? ....
B: Three years ago.

4 A: How many people / invite / so far? ....
B: Over thirty.

5 A: How often / elections / hold in Great Britain? ....
B: Every five years.

6 A: When / your car / steal? ....
B: Last week.

D Translate the following sentences using the passive.

1 Wie wird dieses Wort ausgesprochen?
2 Wann ist diese Brücke gebaut worden?
3 Gestern sind zehn Leute bei einem Unfall verletzt worden.
4 Eine Entscheidung wird nächste Woche getroffen.
5 Telefonkarten kann man fast überall kaufen.

22 The passive (2)
Das Passiv (2)

A: What did you see when you went to the film studios?
B: Well, ~~us was given~~ we were given a guided tour of the whole place.
A: That sounds good.
B: And ~~us was shown~~ we were shown how they make an episode of a soap opera.
A: Really? I bet that was interesting.
B: Yes, it was. Actually, the Christmas episode ~~was just made~~ was just being made.

Verlaufsform im Passiv

- Die Verlaufsform des Passivs bildet man mit einer Form von be + being + Partizip Perfekt. Wie im Aktiv kennzeichnet die Verlaufsform etwas als im Verlauf begriffen, andauernd, nicht abgeschlossen, vorübergehend.

Verlaufsform der Gegenwart	Tim had an accident last week. His car is now at the garage.
Aktiv: am/are/is ...ing	They are repairing it.
Passiv: am/are/is + being + Partizip Perfekt	It is being repaired. *Es wird (gerade) repariert.*
Verlaufsform der Vergangenheit	When we arrived, the hotel still wasn't finished.
Aktiv: was/were ...ing	They were still painting the rooms.
Passiv: was/were + being + Partizip Perfekt	The rooms were still being painted. *Die Zimmer wurden noch gestrichen.*

Das Passiv bei Verben mit zwei Objekten

- Bestimmte Verben können zwei Objekte haben: ein direktes Objekt (meist eine Sache, die gegeben, geschickt usw. wird) und ein indirektes (meist eine Person, der etwas gegeben, geschickt usw. wird).
  My mother gave *me* this ring on my 18th birthday.
  We have shown *him* all 30 photos, but he doesn't recognize the man.

- In Passivsätzen mit solchen Verben kann – im Gegensatz zum Deutschen – auch die Person Subjekt des Satzes werden.
  I (~~Me~~) was given this ring by my mother. *Mir wurde dieser Ring von meiner Mutter geschenkt.*
  = This ring was given *to me* by my mother. *Dieser Ring wurde mir von meiner Mutter geschenkt.*
  He has (~~Him have~~) been shown all 30 photos. *Ihm sind alle 30 Fotos gezeigt worden. / Man hat ihm ... gezeigt.*
  = All 30 photos have been shown *to him*. *Alle 30 Fotos sind ihm gezeigt worden. / Man hat ihm ... gezeigt.*

- Zu den Verben, bei denen die Person Subjekt eines Passivsatzes werden kann, zählen u.a. folgende:
  ask buy give lend offer pay promise sell send show teach tell

! Bei den Verben describe, explain, report und suggest kann nur eine Sache ~~Subjekt des Passivsatzes sein.~~
They explained the problem *to us*. The problem was explained *to us*. ~~We were explained the problem.~~

who-Fragen im Passiv mit by

- Satzstellung: by steht am Satzende, nicht am Satzanfang.
  Who were these photos taken by? *Von wem wurden diese Fotos gemacht?*
  Who was the book written by? *Von wem wurde das Buch geschrieben?*

Das Wichtigste in Kürze

- is being watched, were being cooked usw. = Passiv-Verlaufsform (für etwas, das im Gange ist)
- I was given = „~~Mir~~ wurde gegeben": Person ist Subjekt von Passivsatz bei give, send, show, tell usw.
- Who is this by (from)? = „Von wem ist das (geschrieben/komponiert usw.)?": by steht am Satzende

A One sentence has a mistake. Which sentence is correct?

a The bridge was closed yesterday because it was repaired.
b The bridge was closed yesterday because it was being repaired. ✔

1 **a** Who was this church built by?
b By who was this church built?

2 **a** Can I help you or are you served?
b Can I help you or are you being served?

3 **a** He has been asked to make a speech.
b Him has been asked to make a speech.

4 **a** A new shopping centre is built there.
b A new shopping centre is being built there.

5 **a** Your car isn't ready, sir. It is still repaired.
b Your car isn't ready, sir. It is still being repaired.

6 **a** I was given a warm welcome when I arrived.
b I was being given a warm welcome when I arrived.

B Make passive sentences or questions.

Last year they sent her to the Berlin office for two months.
Last year she *was sent to the Berlin office for two months.*

1 Nobody told me about the meeting.

I ……………………………………………………………………………………

2 How much did they pay you?

How much ……………………………………………………………………………

3 Has anyone explained the new computer program to you?

Has the computer program ……………………………………………………………

4 They will show the royal wedding on TV.

The royal wedding ……………………………………………………………………

5 Someone must write the letter this week.

The letter ……………………………………………………………………………

6 They have asked me to help at the school Christmas party.

I ……………………………………………………………………………………

C Make passive questions for these answers.

Who / the new concert hall / open / last week? – By the Queen.
Who was the new concert hall opened by last week?

1 David / offer / a place at university yet? – No, not yet.

2 Why / the flight / cancel / yesterday? – Because of fog.

3 When / the book / be published? – Next year.

4 What / build / here? – A new school. It's nearly finished.

5 Who / this book / write? – By Agatha Christie.

D Translate the following sentences.

1 Unsere neue Couch ist gerade geliefert (*deliver*) worden.
2 Letzte Woche wurde mir eine Stelle in einer anderen Abteilung angeboten.
3 Kann ich Ihnen helfen? – Nein danke. Ich werde schon bedient.
4 Als wir gestern im Hotel ankamen, wurde unser Zimmer gerade geputzt.
5 Zurzeit wird alles gemacht, um das Problem zu lösen.

23 Modal verbs (1): can
Modalverben (1): can

A: How was the French holiday?
B: Fine. I ~~can to sail~~ *can sail* now. I did a course there.
A: With a French trainer?
B: Yes, but she spoke English. ~~Can you French?~~ *Can you speak French?*
A: No, I can't. But a lot of French people speak English, don't they?
B: Yes, they do. One day I needed some medicine at a chemist's and ~~could~~ *was able to* ask for it in English.

Deutsch „können“: can, be able to

- **can** hat keine Present Perfect- oder Zukunftsform. Diese werden mit dem Ersatzverb **be able to** gebildet.

Gegenwart	I **can** speak French. I **can't** speak Italian. *kann (nicht)*
Vergangenheit	At six she **could** read. She **couldn't** swim. *konnte (nicht)*
	He **was able to** call the police because he had a mobile phone with him.
Present Perfect	I **have been able to** find Tom. I **haven't been able to** find Jill. *habe (nicht) können*
Zukunft	We **will be able to** meet. We **won't be able to** talk long. *werden (nicht) können*

- Auf **can/can't** folgt ein Infinitiv ohne **to**.

- In der Vergangenheit gebraucht man für eine generelle Fähigkeit meist **could**.
  I **could swim** when I was four.

! Wenn gesagt wird, was jemandem in einer Einzelsituation gelang, muss man **was/were able to** gebrauchen. In Fragen und verneinten Sätzen ist **could** jedoch ebenfalls möglich.
Luckily I **was able to** (~~could~~) **find** a shop that was still open.
Could you **find** / **Were** you **able to find** a shop that was still open?
I **couldn't find** / **wasn't able to find** a shop that was still open.

- **can** wird gebraucht, wenn man jetzt etwas für die Zukunft anbietet oder vorschlägt.
  Today is not possible, but we **can meet** tomorrow if you like.

! Nur **will be able to** ist möglich, wenn die Fähigkeit, etwas zu tun, jetzt noch nicht vorhanden ist.
He's broken his leg, but he **will be able to** (~~can~~) **walk** again soon.

- **can** kann – außer z.B. in Kurzantworten – nicht allein stehen (d.h. ohne ein weiteres Verb).
  I **can speak** French (~~can French~~). *Ich kann Französisch.*
  I don't cook very often. My husband **can do** it (~~can it~~) better. *Mein Mann kann es besser.*

Verben der Sinneswahrnehmung

- Verben der Sinneswahrnehmung – **see**, **hear**, **smell**, **taste**, **touch** – stehen meist mit **can** oder **could**, wenn man eine momentane Wahrnehmung ausdrückt.
  I **can see/hear/smell** the sea. *Ich sehe/höre/rieche das Meer.*
  I **could taste** something bitter in the soup. *Ich schmeckte etwas Bitteres in der Suppe.*

Das Wichtigste in Kürze

- **can** hat nur zwei Formen: **can** (Gegenwart) und **could** (Vergangenheit); andere Zeitstufen: **be able to**
- „konnte(n)“ (Vergangenheit) = **could** nur in Allgemeinaussagen; einmaliges Gelingen = **was/were able to**
- „können“ mit Zukunftsbezug = **can** bei Angeboten und Vorschlägen; sicherer ist sonst **will be able to**
- **see**, **hear**, **smell**, **taste**, **touch**: mit **can/could** bei momentaner Sinneswahrnehmung

Weitere Informationen → Unit 25

A One sentence has a mistake. Which sentence is correct?

a I can understand more after my course in London next month.
b I'll be able to understand more after my course in London next month. ✔

1 **a** I could see Tom when I was in London.
b I was able to see Tom when I was in London.

2 **a** What see you in the picture?
b What can you see in the picture?

3 **a** Will you be able to come later? – Yes, I will.
b Will you be able to come later? – Yes, I be able.

4 **a** My sister can Spanish.
b My sister can speak Spanish.

5 **a** Were you able to go to Jane's party? – Yes, I was.
b Was you able to go to Jane's party? – Yes, I was.

6 **a** I can come tomorrow.
b I can to come tomorrow.

B Complete the answers to these questions using can/can't, could/couldn't or a form of be able to.

1 A: Did you get the chance to go to the Opera House when you were in Sydney?
B: Yes, we were so lucky! We .... get tickets for a modern ballet.

2 A: Have you invited Carol and Jane to the party?
B: Well, I left a message on Carol's answering machine yesterday but I .... speak to Jane yet – perhaps she's away.

3 A: How was your concert yesterday – it was the first performance, wasn't it?
B: It went well but I was so nervous. I .... enjoy it!

4 A: How does your sister feel about her husband's new job in the States?
B: Well, she's a bit worried about finding work herself. She .... work when she's got a green card.

5 A: What was your hotel like?
B: Fantastic. We had a wonderful view. We .... see the sea from our window.

C Make questions for these answers. Use can, could or a form of be able to.

1 A: .... French?
B: No, I can't really. I only had French lessons for a couple of years at school.

2 A: .... when you were a child?
B: No, I couldn't. I learned to swim when I was forty.

3 A: How was the flight? .... on the plane?
B: Yes, I was. I slept really well.

4 A: Doctor, how bad is my son's injury? .... football again?
B: Yes, I'm sure he will. But he must be patient – it will take time.

D Translate the following sentences.

1 Konnten Sie letztes Wochenende im Garten arbeiten oder war das Wetter zu schlecht?
2 Ich sehe die Berge aus meinem Fenster.
3 Es tut mir leid. Ich habe deinen Brief noch nicht übersetzen können.
4 Hilf mir bitte. Ich kann es nicht alleine (*on my own*).
5 Hast du schon mit deinem Chef sprechen können?

24 Modal verbs (2): must
Modalverben (2): must

A: Back from the dentist already?
B: Yes, I ~~hadn't to~~ *didn't have to* wait long.
A: What did she say? Are your teeth OK?
B: Well, she ~~must~~ *had to* put a new filling in this tooth here.
A: Oh. But the other teeth are OK?
B: Yes, I ~~mustn't~~ *needn't / don't have to* go back again till next year.

Deutsch „müssen": must, have to

- must hat keine Vergangenheits-, Present Perfect- oder Zukunftsform. Das Ersatzverb ist have to.

Gegenwart	I must call / have to call Bill. *Ich muss Bill anrufen.*
Vergangenheit	We had to (~~must~~) phone the doctor. *Wir mussten den Arzt anrufen.*
Present Perfect	I have/haven't had to do this often. *Das habe ich (nicht) oft machen müssen.*
Zukunft	You will/won't have to wait. *Sie werden (nicht) warten müssen.*

mustn't – needn't – don't have to

- „nicht müssen" wird durch needn't (= nicht brauchen) oder durch don't/doesn't have to ausgedrückt.
  I needn't go / don't have to (~~mustn't~~) go yet. *Ich muss noch nicht gehen. / Ich brauche noch nicht zu gehen.*

! must not entspricht „nicht dürfen"! Vgl.:
You needn't worry. *Du musst dir keine Sorgen machen. / Du brauchst dir keine Sorgen zu machen.*
I don't have to work on Thursday. It's a holiday. *Ich muss … nicht arbeiten./Ich brauche … nicht zu arbeiten.*
I mustn't forget. It's Ann's birthday tomorrow. *Ich darf es nicht vergessen.*

Fragen und Verneinung mit have to

- Verneinung und Fragen mit have to bildet man in der Gegenwart und Vergangenheit mit einer Form von do.

I don't have to go yet. – Does Ann have to go? – Yes, she does. / No, she doesn't.
We didn't have to wait long. – Did you have to call the police? – Yes, we did. / No, we didn't.

must oder have to in der Gegenwart?

- Der Gebrauch von must und have to überlappt sich in der Gegenwart.
  Fehler vermeidet man, wenn man wie folgt verfährt.
  Befehl: must
  Parent: You must be home by 9.30. All bags must be left at reception.

  Man drückt seine eigenen Gefühle (= innere Überzeugung) aus: must
  We must meet more often. I must give up smoking.

  Man berichtet lediglich, was von anderen angeordnet wird/wurde: have to
  Child: My dad is awful. I have to be home by 9.30.
  We have to pay at the machine before we fetch the car.

  Fragen: have to
  Do we have to pay now? Where do we have to park?

Das Wichtigste in Kürze

- must nur in Gegenwart, sonst have to
- „nicht müssen" = needn't; mustn't = „nicht dürfen"
- have to: Frage und Verneinung mit do
- must = „ich bestimme das" oder „ich halte das für nötig"; have to = „das wird von außen so bestimmt"

Zu amerikanischem Gebrauch siehe Seite 103

A One sentence has a mistake. Which sentence is correct?

a I didn't have to work late yesterday. ✔
b I hadn't to work late yesterday.

1 **a** I mustn't forget to post these letters.
b I don't have to forget to post these letters.

2 **a** You needn't come if you don't have time.
b You mustn't come if you don't have time.

3 **a** Where have we to buy our tickets?
b Where do we have to buy our tickets?

4 **a** Does Ann have to work tomorrow? – Yes, she does.
b Does Ann have to work tomorrow? – Yes, she has.

5 **a** You don't have to smoke on the underground.
b You mustn't smoke on the underground.

6 **a** Had you to wait long at the doctor's?
b Did you have to wait long at the doctor's?

B Complete these sentences with musn't or don't/doesn't have to.

You *mustn't* be late.

1 My husband .... go to hospital. Thank goodness!

2 You .... tell anyone what I told you. It's a secret.

3 I .... go to work tomorrow.

4 I .... forget to go to the bank.

5 You .... wash that pullover in the washing machine. It says 'hand wash only'.

6 My sister .... worry about money. Her husband is very rich.

C Make questions for these answers. Use a form of have to.

A: *Did you have to* wait long?
B: No, I didn't. Jane's train was on time.

1 A: What time does the concert start? When .... leave?

B: Well, we shouldn't leave too late otherwise we won't get a parking space.

2 A: .... work last weekend?

B: No, I didn't, but I have to work next weekend.

3 A: .... go now?

B: Yes, I'm sorry, I do. I have to get up so early tomorrow.

4 A: Do you think we .... open our suitcases when we get to Moscow?

B: Well, the last time I was there we did.

5 A: .... do a written test at any of the interviews you've been to?

B: No, I haven't. So far they've just asked me a few questions to test my French.

D Translate the following sentences.

1 Ich muss wirklich mehr Grammatik lernen.
2 Hast du genügend Pfund im Urlaub gehabt oder musstest du mehr umtauschen?
3 Mein Arzt ist gut, aber man muss immer warten.
4 Müssen wir mitkommen?
5 Morgen muss ich nicht arbeiten.

25 Modal verbs (3): can, may, might, could
Modalverben (3): can, may, might, could

A: I see it's raining again.

B: Yes, but it's still early. It ~~can~~ may/might/could clear up later.

A: I was planning to go to the sea.

B: Well, the weather ~~couldn't~~ may not / might not be so bad down there. It's often better on the coast.

A: Yes. Actually, if I go, could I borrow your new camera?

B: Yes, you ~~could~~ can/may. But be careful with it, please.

Erlaubnis ausdrücken

- **can oder may wird gebraucht, um eine höfliche Bitte zu stellen oder um Erlaubnis zu geben bzw. zu verweigern. May ist eher förmlich.**

  Can/May I open the window, please? – Yes, of course you can/may. / No, I'm sorry, you can't/may not.
  You wanted to borrow my printer. OK, you can/may.

- **could ist in Bitten ebenfalls möglich, wird aber nicht gebraucht, um Erlaubnis zu erteilen bzw. zu verweigern.**

  Could I look at your map, please? – Yes, you can/may (~~could~~).
  I'm sorry, but you can't (~~couldn't~~) park here. This is private.

Möglichkeit und Ungewissheit ausdrücken

- **Mit may/might/could (aber nicht ~~can~~) drückt man aus, dass etwas möglicherweise der Fall ist / sein wird.**

  A: The phone's ringing.
  B: It may/might/could (~~can~~) be for me. I'm expecting a call. *Es kann/könnte für mich sein.*

  A: How much will the repair cost?
  B: I don't know. But it may/might/could (~~can~~) be quite expensive. *Es kann/könnte ziemlich teuer werden.*

- **Mit may/might not (nicht ~~can't/couldn't~~) drückt man aus, dass etwas möglicherweise nicht der Fall ist.**

  A: The phone is ringing. Aren't you going to answer it?
  B: It may/might not be for me. Perhaps it's for you. [= Es könnte sein, dass der Anruf nicht für mich ist.]

  Vergleiche dagegen:
  A: Look, the postman's coming with a big parcel. Are you expecting something?
  B: No, it can't/couldn't be for me. I'm not expecting anything.
  [= Es kann nicht sein / Es ist ausgeschlossen, dass das Paket für mich ist.]

Das Wichtigste in Kürze

- **Um Erlaubnis bitten („darf ich?"): can? may? oder could?**
- **Erlaubnis erteilen und verweigern („du darfst/darfst nicht"): can('t), may (not); aber nicht ~~could (not)~~**
- **„das ist möglicherweise der Fall / das kann sein": may, might, could; aber nicht ~~can~~**
- **„das ist möglicherweise nicht der Fall / es kann sein, dass das nicht der Fall ist": may not, might not; aber nicht ~~can't~~, ~~couldn't~~**

A One sentence has a mistake. Which sentence is correct?

a I'm not sure – the hotel can be more expensive in the high season.
b I'm not sure – the hotel may be more expensive in the high season. ✔

1 **a** May I to smoke, please?
b May I smoke, please?

2 **a** Sue can know Jane's new address.
b Sue might know Jane's new address.

3 **a** That book can't be mine. I left mine at home.
b That book may not be mine. I left mine at home.

4 **a** Could I go now, please? – Yes, you can, of course.
b Could I go now, please? – Yes, you could, of course.

5 **a** That might be for me – I've ordered a pizza.
b That can be for me – I've ordered a pizza.

6 **a** Sue doesn't may come this evening.
b Sue may not come this evening.

B Which sentences are correct: a, b, or a and b?

a I may be late this evening. ✔
b I might be late this evening. ✔

1 **a** Can I borrow your dictionary, please?
b May I borrow your dictionary, please?

2 **a** Where's John? – I don't know. He can be at lunch.
b Where's John? – I don't know. He may be at lunch.

3 **a** Could I bring my sister to your party on Saturday? – Yes, you can – no problem.
b Can I bring my sister to your party on Saturday? – Yes, you can – no problem.

4 **a** Who's Sally talking to? – I'm not sure. It can be her sister.
b Who's Sally talking to? – I'm not sure. It could be her sister.

5 **a** That phone call may be for me. Sue said she would ring about 10 o'clock.
b That phone call might be for me. Sue said she would ring about 10 o'clock.

C Complete the dialogues using can, can't or may (not).

A: Can I use your phone, please? B: Yes, of course you *can*.

1 A: Who's that at the door?
B: It .... be Tom. He said he'd call round if he had time.

2 A: That person over there looks just like Dave. Is it his brother?
B: No, it .... be. Dave hasn't got any brothers or sisters.

3 A: What's the matter? You .... be tired – you went to bed so early yesterday!
B: I don't know. It .... be the air in this room.

4 A: Drive carefully. The roads .... be icy.
B: Well, I .... go by car anyway. It's probably safer by train.

5 A: .... I borrow this book, please?
B: Of course, you can. You .... take this one too if you like.

D Translate the following sentences. Use can, can't, could, may or might.

1 Darf ich das Fenster zumachen?
2 Es tut mir leid, aber Sie können Ihr Fahrrad hier nicht lassen.
3 Könnte ich später zurückrufen? – Natürlich können Sie das.
4 Der Brief könnte von Paul sein – er wollte mir schreiben.
5 Nimm einen Regenschirm. Vielleicht regnet es später.

26 Gerund (1): verb + ...ing
Gerundium (1): Verb + ...ing

A: What shall we do this evening?

B: I suggest ~~to stay~~ *staying* at home.

A: Not again. You're so boring. Come on, let's go to the pub.

B: I don't like ~~that we go~~ *going* to the pub all the time. You just want to see all your football mates.

A: No, no. I want to go there with you.

B: I don't believe you. Can't you imagine ~~to stay~~ *staying* at home and ~~watch~~ *watching* a nice video?

Gerundium = Nomen

- **Das Gerundium ist ein Nomen, das aus einem Verb abgeleitet wird. Es hat die Endung -ing. Wie andere Nomen kann das Gerundium ein Subjekt sein.**

  Sport is good for you. Swimming is good for you. *Sport ist gesund. Schwimmen ist gesund.*

Gerundium nach bestimmten Verben

- **Das Gerundium steht als Objekt nach bestimmten Verben.**

  I've left the choir. I miss singing. *Ich bin aus dem Chor ausgetreten. Ich vermisse das Singen.*

  I have to practise parking for my driving test. *Ich muss das Einparken für meine Fahrprüfung üben.*

! **Oft entspricht die -ing-Form (Gerundium) einem Infinitiv im Deutschen.**

Can you imagine living (~~to live~~) in Alaska? *Kannst du dir vorstellen, in Alaska zu leben?*

You risk losing (~~to lose~~) all your money. *Du riskierst, dein ganzes Geld zu verlieren.*

I suggest leaving (~~to leave~~) early. *Ich schlage vor, früh loszufahren.*

Do you mind waiting (~~to wait~~)? *Macht es Ihnen etwas aus zu warten?*

- **Verb + ...ing wird z.T. im Deutschen auch anders wiedergegeben.**

  I like cooking / driving / travelling. *Ich koche gern / fahre gern Auto / reise gern.*

  He kept (on) / carried on asking the same questions. *Er stellte immer wieder die gleichen Fragen.*

  Have you finished eating? *Sind Sie mit dem Essen fertig?*

- **Zu den Verben, auf die ein Gerundium folgt, zählen insbesondere folgende.**

like* *gern haben/tun*	start* *anfangen*	admit *zugeben*
love* *sehr gern haben/tun*	begin* *beginnen*	avoid *vermeiden*
enjoy *gern haben/tun*	continue *weiter tun*	imagine *sich vorstellen*
dislike *ungern haben/tun*	carry on *weiter tun*	mention *erwähnen*
hate* *sehr ungern haben/tun*	keep (on) *weiter tun*	miss *vermissen*
prefer* *lieber haben/tun*	finish *zu Ende tun*	practise *üben*
(not) mind *etwas/nichts dagegen haben*	stop *aufhören*	recommend *empfehlen*
	give up *aufgeben*	suggest *vorschlagen*

Auf die mit * gekennzeichneten Verben (in dieser Bedeutung) kann auch ein Infinitiv folgen.

! **Auf would like (*möchte/n*), would love (*würde/n liebend gern*), would prefer (*würde/n lieber*), would hate (*würde/n sehr ungern*) folgt immer ein to-Infinitiv.**

I'd like to ask (~~asking~~) a question. *Ich möchte eine Frage stellen.*

- **Auf viele andere Verben folgt ebenfalls – wie im Deutschen – immer ein Infinitiv, z.B. decide, hope, learn, plan, want, offer, promise, afford (*sich leisten*), manage (*es schaffen*).**

Das Wichtigste in Kürze

- **...ing nach bestimmten Verben, insbesondere Verben des Mögens und Nicht-Mögens und Verben, die Beginnen, Fortsetzen und Beenden ausdrücken**

Weitere Informationen → Units 27-30

A One sentence has a mistake. Which sentence is correct?

a My father has given up to smoke.
b My father has given up smoking. ✔

1 **a** I suggest to meet at six o'clock.
b I suggest meeting at six o'clock.

2 **a** Could you imagine to live in the USA?
b Could you imagine living in the USA?

3 **a** We would like to go to Canada next year.
b We would like going to Canada next year.

4 **a** Jane can't afford to go on holiday this year.
b Jane can't afford going on holiday this year.

5 **a** I don't mind to help you at the weekend.
b I don't mind helping you at the weekend.

6 **a** I've managed to find the book you wanted.
b I've managed finding the book you wanted.

B Rewrite these sentences using the gerund.

Sue said, "Let's go to the cinema."
Sue suggested *going to the cinema.*

1 Paul said, "We can go to the theatre if you want."
Paul said he didn't mind ....
2 Joe said, "I stole the bike."
Joe admitted ....
3 Jenny said, "I think it would be nice to live in Australia."
Jenny said she could imagine ....
4 Mary, "You should book early at the new Indian restaurant."
Mary recommended ....
5 Dave, "I saw Carol at the party."
Dave mentioned ....
6 Jane, "I don't go to work by car any more."
Jane has stopped ....

C Complete these dialogues using the gerund or the infinitive.

A: Carol has suggested *going* (go) to the theatre on Saturday.
B: I really don't want *to go* (go) out. I'd prefer *to spend* (spend) the evening at home.

1 A: What have you decided .... (do) about your job?
B: I'm going to carry on .... (work) here at the moment. Of course, I'd like .... (have) more money, but I haven't managed .... (speak) to the boss yet.
2 A: Would you mind .... (turn off) the TV, please? I can't concentrate.
B: Then I suggest .... (go) into the dining room to work! You know I want .... (watch) this programme.
3 A: I think we should leave early tomorrow to avoid .... (drive) in the rush hour.
B: You know I hate .... (get up) early. I'd prefer .... (go) when the rush hour's over.
4 A: Have you learned .... (use) the new software yet?
B: Unfortunately not, but my boss has promised .... (send) me on a course.
5 A: We can't afford .... (go) abroad for a holiday this year, so we've planned .... (go) camping.
B: I'm sure you'll miss .... (have) a comfortable bed – I can't imagine you .... (sleep) in a tent!

D Translate the following sentences.

1 Ich schlage vor, der Firma einen Brief zu schreiben.
2 Mein Nachbar hat angeboten, mein Auto zu reparieren.
3 Ich kann mir nicht vorstellen, diese Gegend zu verlassen, aber meine Frau will umziehen.
4 Wir möchten einen Tisch reservieren. Wir sitzen gerne am Fenster.
5 Sue und Tom haben versprochen, pünktlich zu sein.

27 Gerund (2): preposition + ...ing
Gerundium (2): Präposition + ...ing

A: I see you've got an invitation to a class reunion: "Class 6B 15 years later".

B: Yes. I'm looking forward to ~~see~~ seeing my old school friends again.

A: Where is it?

B: At the school. Someone had the idea ~~to eat~~ of eating in the school canteen!

A: That doesn't sound a very good idea.

B: I'm thinking about ~~to take~~ taking a picnic with me!

Gerundium nach Präpositionen

- **Nach einer Präposition (about, against, at, in, of, on usw.) steht ein Verb immer in der -ing-Form. Die Präposition bildet oft mit einem Adjektiv, Nomen oder Verb eine Einheit.**

- Adjektiv + Präposition + ...ing
  She's **good/bad at persuading** people. *Sie kann Leute gut/schlecht überzeugen.*
  I was **afraid/frightened of making** a mistake. *Ich hatte Angst, einen Fehler zu machen.*
  I'm **tired of** / I'm **fed up with visiting** museums. *Ich habe es satt, Museen zu besuchen.*
  I'm **interested in meeting** him. *Ich habe Lust / bin daran interessiert, ihn kennenzulernen.*

- Nomen + Präposition + ...ing
  What is the **advantage of paying** now? *Welchen Vorteil / Welche Vorteile hat es, jetzt zu zahlen?*
  What are the **chances of finding** a taxi? *Wie stehen die Chancen, ein Taxi zu finden?*
  I hate the **idea/thought of paying** so much. *... die Idee / den Gedanken, so viel zu bezahlen.*
  There are good **reasons for eating** a lot of fruit. *Es gibt gute Gründe dafür, viel Obst zu essen.*

- Verb + Präposition + ...ing
  He **talked/spoke/dreamed about emigrating**. *Er sprach/träumte davon auszuwandern.*
  I **thought about/of asking** Tim for help. *Ich dachte daran, Tim um Hilfe zu bitten.*
  I **decided against** / I **am against moving**. *Ich entschied mich dagegen / bin dagegen, umzuziehen.*
  He **apologized for being** late. *Er entschuldigte sich dafür, dass er sich verspätet hatte.*
  She **thanked** us **for helping** her. *Sie dankte uns dafür, dass wir ihr geholfen hatten.*
  We **succeeded in persuading** her. *Es gelang uns, sie zu überzeugen.*
  She **insisted on paying** for everybody. *Sie bestand darauf, für alle zu bezahlen.*

!

Auch nach look forward to, be used to und object to folgt eine -ing-Form, kein Infinitiv!
I'm **looking forward to meeting** (~~meet~~) him again. *Ich freue mich darauf, ihn wiederzusehen.*
In Norway we **are used to having** (~~have~~) a lot of snow. *In ... sind wir es gewöhnt, ... zu haben.*
They **objected to sitting** (~~sit~~) in the smoking section. *Sie protestierten dagegen, ... zu sitzen.*

- **Eine -ing-Form wird auch nach How/What about?, be worth und feel like gebraucht.**
  How/What about going to the cinema this evening? *Wie wäre es, wenn wir ... ins Kino gingen?*
  It'**s (not) worth waiting**. *Es lohnt sich (nicht) zu warten.*
  I **feel like going** for a walk. *Ich hätte Lust, spazieren zu gehen.*

- **before, after, by, instead of und without stehen allein mit einer -ing-Form.**
  Before opening the letter, she took a deep breath. *Bevor sie ... öffnete, atmete sie tief durch.*
  You can save 10% **by booking** on the Internet. *Man kann 10% sparen, wenn man ... bucht.*
  Instead of waiting, I went to another shop. *Anstatt zu warten, ging ich in einen anderen Laden.*
  She left **without saying** goodbye. *Sie fuhr weg, ohne sich zu verabschieden.*

Das Wichtigste in Kürze

- **Nach einer Präposition: -ing-Form, nicht Infinitiv!**

Weitere Informationen → Units 28-30

A One sentence has a mistake. Which sentence is correct?

a I'm not interested for learning another language.
b I'm not interested in learning another language. ✔

1 **a** Are you good in making decisions?
b Are you good at making decisions?

2 **a** Ed got the job without having an interview.
b Ed got the job without to have an interview.

3 **a** We're looking forward to go on holiday.
b We're looking forward to going on holiday.

4 **a** We're thinking about to look for a new flat.
b We're thinking about looking for a new flat.

5 **a** What's the advantage from booking a return ticket?
b What's the advantage of booking a return ticket?

6 **a** It's not worth to book early.
b It's not worth booking early.

B Rewrite these sentences with the gerund and the correct preposition.

I'm fed up with learning vocabulary.
I'm tired *of learning vocabulary*.

1 Sandra doesn't mind working on Saturdays.
Sandra is used ....

2 I'd like to meet your new boss.
I'm interested ....

3 We're not going to buy a new kitchen.
We've decided ....

4 We managed to find a parking space.
We succeeded ....

5 I didn't want John to help me, but he did.
John insisted ....

6 I don't want to leave so early.
I object ....

C Complete the dialogues with the gerund (+ correct preposition) or the infinitive.

A: The thought *of moving* (move) is terrible.
B: I know. I don't want *to go* (go) either.

1 A: The chances .... (get) a last-minute holiday are not very good.
B: Well, we can't afford .... (pay) the full price.

2 A: You're really good .... (remember) names. What's the name of that new restaurant we went to last month? I'm thinking .... (book) a table for Saturday. Would you like .... (come) with us?
B: No, thanks. I don't feel like .... (go) out at the weekend.

3 A: My goodness, I'm exhausted! I'm not used .... (jog) so far. I'm looking forward .... (have) a shower and a rest.
B: You wanted .... (run) round the lake! I suggested .... (take) a shorter route but you insisted .... (come) this way!

4 A: What about .... (buy) Jane a picture for her birthday?
B: I'd prefer .... (get) her some clothes. I'm thinking .... (buy) her a pullover.

D Translate the following sentences using the gerund and, where necessary, the correct preposition.

1 Wir haben uns ein Boot gekauft, statt in Urlaub zu fahren.
2 Paul ist dagegen, ein neues Auto zu kaufen.
3 Sue kann Grammatik gut erklären.
4 Ich habe Angst davor, zum Zahnarzt zu gehen.
5 Wir freuen uns, euch nächste Woche zu sehen.

28 Infinitive
Infinitiv

A: What are you doing with that big saucepan?

B: I promised ~~lending~~ to lend it to Don. He's cooking for 30 people for a party.

A: Hasn't he got his own saucepans?

B: Yes, but not a big one. It would mean ~~to buy~~ buying one just for this party.

A: Well, I need it. I'm cooking for Tina's kindergarten on Monday.

B: Don's party is on Saturday, so he can give it back on Sunday. I'll remember ~~telling~~ to tell him.

Verb + Infinitiv

- Auf viele Verben folgt ein Infinitiv mit **to**.

I **want to go** now. *Ich will jetzt gehen.*
We can't **afford to go** on holiday. *Wir können es uns nicht leisten, in Urlaub zu fahren.*

afford *sich leisten*	**expect** *damit rechnen*	**offer** *anbieten*	**seem** *scheinen*
agree *sich einigen*	**hope** *hoffen*	**plan** *planen*	**try** *versuchen*
decide *beschließen, sich entscheiden*	**learn** *lernen*	**promise** *versprechen*	**want** *wollen*
	manage *es schaffen*	**refuse** *sich weigern*	

Verb + Infinitiv oder Gerundium

- Auf einige Verben folgt ohne Bedeutungsunterschied ein Infinitiv oder ein Gerundium.

I **started/began to yawn / yawning**. *Ich fing an zu gähnen.*
I **like/love to lie / lying** in bed. *Ich liege (sehr) gern im Bett.*
We **hate to get / getting** up early. *Wir stehen sehr ungern früh auf.*
We **prefer to drink / drinking** tea. *Wir trinken lieber Tee.*

- Bei einigen Verben ergibt sich ein Bedeutungsunterschied.

I must **remember to phone** Ann. *Ich muss daran denken, Ann anzurufen.*
I **remember meeting** Ann in London in 1999. *Ich erinnere mich daran, wie ich Ann ... traf.*
I mustn't **forget to phone** New York. *Ich darf nicht vergessen, in New York anzurufen.*
I'll never **forget arriving** in New York. *Ich werde nie vergessen, wie ich in New York ankam.*
I **stopped to light** a cigarette. *Ich blieb stehen, um eine Zigarette anzuzünden.*
I **stopped smoking** last year. *Ich habe letztes Jahr aufgehört zu rauchen.*
I **meant to tell** you. *Ich wollte / hatte vor, es dir zu sagen.*
If we miss that train, it will **mean having to** wait an hour. *Wenn wir diesen Zug verpassen, bedeutet es, dass wir eine Stunde warten müssen.*

Das Wichtigste in Kürze

- Infinitiv *oder* Gerundium möglich:

→ ohne Bedeutungsunterschied: nach **begin**, **start**, **like**, **love**, **hate**, **prefer**
→ mit Bedeutungsunterschied: nach **remember**, **forget**, **stop**, **mean**

Weitere Informationen → Units 29-30

A One sentence has a mistake. Which sentence is correct?

a Did you remember to go to the bank? ✔
b Did you remember going to the bank?

1 a My colleague refused helping me yesterday.
b My colleague refused to help me yesterday.

2 a We've agreed meeting at 8 o'clock.
b We've agreed to meet at 8 o'clock.

3 a A 6 o'clock flight means getting up at 3 o'clock.
b A 6 o'clock flight means to get up at 3 o'clock.

4 a I forgot buying some coffee – I'll get some tomorrow.
b I forgot to buy some coffee – I'll get some tomorrow.

5 a I can remember to feel very upset when my aunt died.
b I can remember feeling very upset when my aunt died.

6 a We got lost so we stopped asking someone the way.
b We got lost so we stopped to ask someone the way.

B Rewrite the following sentences.

I must phone Carol this evening. I must remember *to phone Carol this evening.*

1 Sue wanted to go to the bank but she forgot.
Sue meant ....
2 Once I went to Alaska. I'll never forget it.
I'll never forget ....
3 Have you given up smoking?
Have you stopped ....
4 We met Sue and had coffee together.
We met Sue and stopped ....
5 I'm sure I left my wallet in the living room.
I can remember ....
6 I was very ill when I was ten. It was terrible.
I'll never forget ....

C Complete the following dialogues with the gerund or the infinitive.

A: Do you expect *to win* (win) your match tomorrow?
B: Not really. I can only remember *winning* (win) once against Jan because he was injured!

1 A: My son is learning .... (drive). He hopes .... (take) his test next month.
B: I'll never forget .... (take) my driving test. I was so nervous but I managed .... (pass) without any problems.

2 A: Where are my keys? I can remember .... (leave) them in the kitchen but they're not there now.
B: The last time you lost them, I suggested .... (leave) them by the front door.

3 A: I meant .... (tell) you about my neighbours last time I saw you. They wrote to the landlord and told him they couldn't afford .... (pay) so much rent and he agreed .... (reduce) it!
B: I'd never think of .... (do) that, but it's worth .... (try).

4 A: Are you enjoying .... (have) more time for yourself now you've stopped .... (work) in London?
B: Yes, working here means .... (not have to) spend hours on commuter trains.

D Translate the following sentences.

1 Ich muss daran denken, zur Bank zu gehen.
2 Wir haben aufgehört, nach einer neuen Wohnung zu suchen. Wir können es uns nicht leisten umzuziehen.
3 Ich hasse es, am Wochenende arbeiten zu müssen.
4 Wo ist mein Wörterbuch? Ich erinnere mich daran, dass ich es Tom ausgeliehen (*lend*) habe.

29 Verb + object + infinitive
Objekt-Infinitiv-Konstruktion

A: What's the matter? Problems with your computer?

B: Yes, I asked Ann ~~help~~ *to help* me. But she's got no time.

A: What's the problem exactly? Can I help?

B: Well, she knows all about computers. I wanted ~~that she installs~~ *her to install* this new software for me.

A: Is that all? I can do that for you. It's easy.

B: Oh thanks. If you have time, I'd like ~~that you check~~ *you to check* the printer for me, too.

Verb + Objekt + to-Infinitiv = deutsch: Verb + Objekt + Infinitiv

- Auf manche Verben folgt ein Objekt + Infinitiv.

  I **asked David to help** me. *Ich bat David, mir zu helfen.*

  She **told me to clean** my shoes. *Sie forderte mich auf, meine Schuhe zu putzen.*

allow *erlauben*	**force** *zwingen*	**order** *befehlen*	**tell** *auffordern*
advise *raten*	**help** *helfen*	**persuade** *überreden*	**warn** *warnen, ermahnen*
ask *bitten*	**invite** *einladen*	**remind** *erinnern*	

! **warn** verwendet man mit **not**, wenn ausgedrückt wird, dass jemand etwas nicht machen soll.

We **warned her not to go** out alone at night. *Wir warnten sie davor, nachts allein auszugehen.*

- Nach **let** (*erlauben*) und **make** (*dazu bringen, zwingen, lassen*) steht der Infinitiv *ohne* **to**.

  My boss **lets me work** at home. *Mein Chef erlaubt mir, zuhause zu arbeiten.*

  What **made her shout** like that? *Was hat sie dazu gebracht, so zu schreien?*

  The teacher **made him write** everything again. *Der Lehrer ließ ihn alles nochmal schreiben.*

Verb + Objekt + Infinitiv = deutsch: Verb + Satz mit „dass/wenn"

! Bei einigen Verben entspricht ein Objekt + Infinitiv einem deutschen Satz mit „dass/wenn".

I **want him to go** now (~~want that he goes now~~). *Ich will, dass er jetzt geht.*

I **expect you to be** on time (~~expect that …~~). *Ich erwarte (= verlange), dass Sie pünktlich sind.*

I **would like you to stay** for dinner (~~would like that …~~). *Ich möchte, dass Sie zum Essen bleiben.*

I **would hate my son to find out** from somebody else (~~would hate that …~~). *Ich hätte es sehr ungern, wenn mein Sohn es von jemand anderem erfahren würde.*

We **are waiting for the rain to stop** (~~waiting that …~~). *Wir warten darauf, dass der Regen aufhört.*

Ein **that**-Satz ist nach diesen Verben im Englischen **nicht** möglich.

Das Wichtigste in Kürze

- Nach **let** und **make**: Infinitiv ohne **to**
- Nach **want**, **(would) like/hate**, **wait for**: **kein** **that**-Satz

Weitere Informationen → Unit 30

A One sentence has a mistake. Which sentence is correct?

a I want go skiing this winter.
b I want to go skiing this winter. ✔

1 a Sue asked the assistant show her some coats.
b Sue asked the assistant to show her some coats.

2 a Sally's parents didn't let her go to the disco.
b Sally's parents didn't let her to go to the disco.

3 a Would you like that I help you?
b Would you like me to help you?

4 a She wanted the children to write an essay.
b She wanted that the children wrote an essay.

5 a I'm waiting for the rush hour to finish before I go.
b I'm waiting that the rush hour finishes before I go.

6 a The man warned his son to play with matches.
b The man warned his son not to play with matches.

B Rewrite the following sentences using the words in brackets and an infinitive.

My father said I had to stay at home last night. **(make/stay)**
My father made me stay at home last night.

1 Dave has invited me to his party. **(would like/come)**

....

2 I need everyone here by nine o'clock. **(expect/be)**

....

3 I told the children that they shouldn't play on the road. **(warn/play)**

....

4 Sue spoke nicely to Jim and he agreed to go to the theatre. **(persuade/go)**

....

5 My mother said I could borrow her car. **(let/borrow)**

....

6 Jane's mother isn't happy with her plan to hitchhike round Europe. **(not want/hitchhike)**

....

C Complete the following questions.

A: Do you want *me to help you* or can you manage alone?
B: It's OK. I don't think I need any help, thanks.

1 A: Would you like .... for you next Saturday?
B: Yes, please. The girl who normally babysits for us is away.

2 A: Can you afford to buy that jacket or do you want .... you some money?
B: Well, could you lend me €100 till next week?

3 A: Didn't you warn Jack .... in front of the neighbours' house?
B: Yes, but he thinks it's OK to park there.

4 A: Can you remind .... Ann this evening, please?
B: Sure. Why do you need to phone her?

5 A: Why did the teacher make .... your homework again?
B: She realized I had copied Sarah's because I had the same mistakes!

D Translate the following sentences.

1 Ich warte darauf, dass jemand die Heizung repariert.
2 Letztes Jahr habe ich meiner Tochter erlaubt, mit einer Freundin in Urlaub zu fahren.
3 Meine Frau will, dass ich zuhause bleibe und auf die Kinder aufpasse.
4 Wir haben dich davor gewarnt, in diese Firma zu investieren.
5 Wir möchten gerne, dass unser Sohn in den Schulferien einen Sprachkurs macht.

30 used to – be/get used to

A: When you start your new job, the journey to work will be quite long, won't it? 60 kilometres?

B: Yes, but I'm used to ~~travel~~ travelling a long way.

A: How far do you travel now? 30?

B: 32. It used to ~~taking~~ take me about 20 minutes, but now it's often nearly 40.

A: Because of the traffic?

B: Yes. Last week I ~~used to take~~ took the train for a few days. But that wasn't any better. It was so full.

used to

- **Mit used to plus Infinitiv sagt man, was man früher gewohnheitsmäßig getan hat – und jetzt nicht mehr tut.**

  I used to smoke, but I stopped two years ago. *Früher habe ich geraucht ...*

  You used to cycle to work. Why have you stopped? *Früher sind Sie zur Arbeit geradelt. ...*

  We used to live in Scotland before Ann got her new job. *Früher lebten wir in Schottland, bis ...*

- **Frage und Verneinung werden mit did(n't) use to gebildet.**

  Did you use to watch Sesame Street as a child? *Hast du als Kind ... geschaut?*

  I drink a lot of green tea. I didn't use to like tea. *... Früher mochte ich keinen Tee.*

be used to – get used to

- **be used to beschreibt eine bestehende Gewohnheit; be used to something entspricht „etwas gewohnt sein".**

  Here in Alaska we're used to cold weather. *Hier in Alaska sind wir kaltes Wetter gewohnt.*

- **get used to beschreibt den Gewöhnungsprozess; get used to something entspricht „sich an etwas gewöhnen".**

  I can't get used to this new uniform. *Ich kann mich an diese neue Uniform nicht gewöhnen.*

! Auf be/get used to folgt ein Gerundium (-ing-Form), kein Infinitiv!

We're used to eating (~~eat~~) late. *Wir sind es gewohnt, spät zu essen.*

He never got used to living (~~live~~) abroad. *Er hat sich nie daran gewöhnt, im Ausland zu leben.*

Vergleiche:

I used to work at nights. *Früher habe ich nachts gearbeitet. [Aber ich tue es nicht mehr.]*

I'm used to working at the weekend. *Ich bin es gewohnt, [jetzt] am Wochenende zu arbeiten.*

Das Wichtigste in Kürze

- used to = vergangene Gewohnheit („früher habe ich immer ... aber jetzt nicht mehr")
  be used to = bestehende Gewohnheit („ich bin ... gewohnt / war damals ... gewohnt")
  get used to = Gewöhnungsprozess („ich gewöhne/gewöhnte mich an ...")
- used to: Frage/Verneinung mit did(n't) use to: Did you use to ... / I didn't use to ...
- be/get used to + ...ing

A One sentence has a mistake. Which sentence is correct?

a Where use you to live before you moved here?
b Where did you use to live before you moved here? ✔

1 **a** It used to taking me an hour to get to work until they built the new motorway.
b It used to take me an hour to get to work until they built the new motorway.

2 **a** I didn't use to like spinach – now it's one of my favourite vegetables.
b I use not to like spinach – now it's one of my favourite vegetables.

3 **a** Jane is used to living in the centre of town – the noise of the traffic doesn't worry her.
b Jane is used to live in the centre of town – the noise of the traffic doesn't worry her.

4 **a** When we were on holiday last month, we hired a car for a few days.
b When we were on holiday last month, we used to hire a car for a few days.

B Complete these dialogues with be used to and the -ing form.

A: Is your daughter happy in her new flat?
B: She's surprised how much work it is! She / not / live alone. *She's not used to living alone.*

1 A: How do you feel about the conference now?

B: Very nervous. I / not / speak in front of so many people. ....

2 A: As a nurse, you must have to work at night. Isn't that hard?

B: No, it's OK. I / work at night. ....

3 A: Your son's penfriend is coming next week, isn't he?

B: Yes, I'll have to cook a proper meal every day. I / not / do that! ....

4 A: Don doesn't look very well. Do you think he's OK?

B: I think he's had too much wine. He / not / drink so much. ....

5 A: Didn't you have problems driving on the left in Cyprus?

B: I did, but my wife comes from England so she / drive on the left. ....

C Complete these sentences by underlining the correct form.

If you move to England, you'll have to get used <u>to driving</u> / to drive on the left.

1 I didn't go to bed until 1 o'clock yesterday. I'm not used to going / to go to bed so late.

2 I thought you had always worked at this bank. I didn't realize you used to working / to work at a hospital.

3 My husband has to work shifts in his new job. He'll have to get used to sleeping / to sleep in the daytime.

4 When we first moved to Spain, we found it difficult to get used to eating / to eat so late in the evening.

5 When we were children, we used to living / to live in Somerset.

D Translate the following sentences. If possible, use used to.

1 Letzte Woche habe ich meinen ersten Pauschalurlaub (*package holiday*) gebucht.
2 Ich habe früher immer gesagt, ich würde nie einen Pauschalurlaub buchen.
3 Als ich jünger war, habe ich nie ein Hotel gebucht, nur den Flug.
4 Ich habe immer gezeltet (*go camping*).
5 Einmal habe ich in einer Pension gewohnt (*stay in a guesthouse*), aber sie war furchtbar.

31 Relative clauses (1)
Relativsätze (1)

A: Was that Sonia in that car?

B: Yes, and the man ~~he~~ who/that was driving was Philip Barnes.

A: Philip Barnes?

B: Yes. He's the person ~~which~~ who/that wants to open that restaurant where the old hat shop was.

A: Oh yes. A new restaurant round here would be a good thing. But how does Sonia know him?

B: Well, I'll tell you something ~~what~~ that happened the other day ...

Relativsätze mit who, which, that, whose

- **In den folgenden zwei Sätzen sind who smoke und which leak Relativsätze.**
  People who smoke live dangerously. *Leute, die rauchen, leben gefährlich.*
  Shoes which leak are useless. *Schuhe, die undicht sind, sind nutzlos.*
  Mit einem Relativsatz bestimmt man Personen oder Sachen genauer.

- **Relativsätze, die Personen genauer bestimmen, werden durch who oder that eingeleitet.**
  Relativsätze, die Sachen genauer bestimmen, werden durch which oder that eingeleitet.
  Is this ***the man*** who/that stole your bag? *Ist das der Mann, der Ihre Tasche gestohlen hat?*
  I need ***a car*** which/that is reliable. *Ich brauche ein Auto, das zuverlässig ist.*
  Diese Relativsätze werden nicht (wie im Deutschen) durch Kommas abgetrennt.

!

that steht auch nach everything, nothing, something und anything.
We threw away everything that (~~what~~) was left. *Wir warfen alles, was übrig blieb, weg.*

Das deutsche „das, was" wird im Englischen nur mit what wiedergegeben.
What (~~That what~~) he said later surprised me. *Das, was er später sagte, überraschte mich.*

- **whose entspricht „dessen/deren".**
  He's the man whose wife had the car accident. *... der Mann, dessen Frau den Autounfall hatte.*
  They're the people whose son lives in Rome. *... die Leute, deren Sohn in Rom lebt.*

Relativsätze ohne Relativpronomen

- **In den folgenden Sätzen ist he und who das Subjekt des Satzes (= derjenige, der schreibt).**

  Tom is that journalist. He writes for the Times.
  Tom is that journalist who writes for the Times. *... der Journalist, der für die Times schreibt.*

- **In den folgenden Sätzen ist we Subjekt des Verbs met; who ist nicht Subjekt, sondern Objekt.**

  Tom is that journalist. ***We*** met him.
  Tom is that journalist who ***we*** met. *... der Journalist, den wir kennengelernt haben.*

- **Wenn das Relativpronomen nicht Subjekt, sondern Objekt ist, kann es weggelassen werden.**
  Tom is that journalist (who/that) ***we*** met on holiday.
  Was that the woman (who/that) ***you*** saw in my office?
  I'm going to wear the pullover (which/that) ***Jenny*** gave me.
  Das Relativpronomen ist nicht Subjekt, sondern Objekt, wenn zwischen who/which/that und dem Verb ein Pronomen oder Nomen steht.

Das Wichtigste in Kürze

- **Personen: who/that – Sachen: which/that**
- **who/which/that kann man weglassen, wenn ein anderes Wort Subjekt des Relativsatzes ist**
- **Relativsätze, die genauer bestimmen, stehen ohne Kommas!**

Weitere Informationen → Unit 32

A One sentence has a mistake. Which sentence is correct?

a The man he is working in the garden is our neighbour.
b The man who is working in the garden is our neighbour. ✔

1 a This is the book what Tom gave me.
b This is the book Tom gave me.

2 a There's the teacher who gives me piano lessons.
b There's the teacher which gives me piano lessons.

3 a That what I have to do in my new job is boring.
b What I have to do in my new job is boring.

4 a That's the person which bought the flat above ours.
b That's the person that bought the flat above ours.

5 a I need a new dress. I haven't got anything that fits.
b I need a new dress. I haven't got anything what fits.

6 a The man who's car was stolen is very angry.
b The man whose car was stolen is very angry.

B Cross out the relative pronouns which are not necessary.

The woman who gives me a lift to work is a neighbour.
The woman ~~who~~ you can see over there is my neighbour.

1 What happened to the paper which I bought yesterday?

2 Those are the people whose daughter sometimes babysits for us.

3 The pullover which you gave me for my birthday fits perfectly.

4 We've just had a letter from the people that we met on holiday.

5 The colleague who helped me move was involved in a car accident yesterday.

6 My boss has asked me to translate some brochures which he got in Spain.

C Where necessary, add the missing relative pronouns.

1 I've just seen the film .... Sarah recommended.

2 What's the name of the teacher .... husband works in Saudi Arabia?

3 .... Tom said about Frank just can't be true.

4 The travel guide .... I bought yesterday contains some good sightseeing tips.

5 What have you done with the keys .... were lying on the kitchen table?

6 Nothing .... happens to Paul surprises me.

D Translate these sentences. If possible, leave out the relative pronouns.

1 Der Mann, der gerade in die Bank geht, ist mein Exchef.
2 Die Leute, die wir auf Janes Party kennengelernt haben, haben gestern Abend angerufen.
3 Heute Abend treffe ich die Freundin, deren Mann Schauspieler und der oft im Fernsehen ist.
4 Ich kann den Film, den wir am Wochenende gesehen haben, wirklich empfehlen.
5 Das, was wir machen müssen, ist nicht sehr einfach.

32 Relative clauses (2)
Relativsätze (2)

A: Have you met Angela Thomas?

B: She's the lady ~~with who you came~~ *you came with*, isn't she?

A: That's right. She's my new boss.

B: I heard that your old boss was leaving, ~~what~~ *which* surprised me.

A: Yes. He's getting married and emigrating to Australia.

B: Really? You know the Bakers, ~~that~~ *who* have been our neighbours for the last 12 years. They're emigrating, too.

Relativsätze mit Präposition

- **In den folgenden Sätzen ist das Relativpronomen nicht Subjekt des Relativsatzes. Es kann also weggelassen werden. Subjekt ist we bzw. I.**

  Ann is the musician. We talked ***to*** her at Jerry's party.
  Ann is the musician (who/that) we talked ***to*** at Jerry's party.
  Ann ist die Musikerin, mit der wir auf Jerrys Party gesprochen haben.

  Here's the camera. I took your picture ***with*** it .
  Here's the camera (which/that) I took your picture ***with***.
  Hier ist der Fotoapparat, mit dem ich das Bild von dir gemacht habe.

  Die Präposition (to, with) steht im Relativsatz an derselben Stelle wie vorher – nicht (wie im Deutschen) vor dem Relativpronomen.

Nicht notwendige Relativsätze mit who, which, whose

- **Ohne den Relativsatz wären die folgenden zwei Sätze unvollständig bzw. ergäben wenig Sinn.**

  Smokers who stop live longer. Cars which have an electric engine are cleaner.

- **Die Relativsätze in den folgenden Sätzen sind dagegen entbehrlich. Sie enthalten Zusatzinformationen, die für das Verständnis nicht notwendig sind.**

  Tony's mother, who by the way smokes like a chimney, is a painter.
  Tonys Mutter, die übrigens wie ein Schlot raucht, ist Malerin.
  The Grand Hotel, which is in fact very small, was closed for repairs.
  Das Grand Hotel, das in Wirklichkeit sehr klein ist, war wegen Reparaturarbeiten geschlossen.

- **Nicht notwendige Relativsätze werden durch who (Personen) oder which (Sachen) eingeleitet, nicht aber durch ~~that~~ ; whose ist auch möglich.**

  Emma, who (~~that~~) has two children, is my best friend.
  Davenport's new book, which (~~that~~) has over 700 pages, is fantastic.
  The Bensons, whose son now lives in Canada, are moving to a smaller house.

  Relativsätze dieser Art werden durch Kommas abgetrennt (wie im Deutschen).

! **which (nicht ~~what~~) leitet entbehrliche Relativsätze ein, die sich auf einen ganzen Satz beziehen.**
Tom didn't phone, which (~~what~~) I found strange. *Tom rief nicht an, was ich seltsam fand.*

Das Wichtigste in Kürze

- **Relativsätze mit Präposition:**
  - who/which/that kann man weglassen
  - die Präposition bleibt hinter dem Verb stehen (wird nicht vor das Relativpronomen gestellt)
- **Nicht notwendige Relativsätze (mit Komma):**
  - who oder which (~~that~~ ist nicht möglich)
  - which, nicht ~~what~~, mit Bezug auf einen ganzen Satz

A One sentence has a mistake. Which sentence is correct?

a What's the name of the person to who you spoke at the travel agent's?
b What's the name of the person you spoke to at the travel agent's? ✔

1 **a** Next year I'm going to visit Lynn, that lives in Boston.
b Next year I'm going to visit Lynn, who lives in Boston.

2 **a** The photo at that Ann is looking was taken in Rome.
b The photo Ann is looking at was taken in Rome.

3 **a** My oldest brother who lives in Sydney has decided to get married.
b My oldest brother, who lives in Sydney, has decided to get married.

4 **a** Tom told a lot of jokes at the dinner party, which got on my nerves.
b Tom told a lot of jokes at the dinner party, what got on my nerves.

B Cross out the relative pronouns which are not necessary.

Where's the dictionary ~~which~~ you were looking at earlier?
How much was the dictionary which was on special offer?

1 That's the man who I bought my car from.

2 That's the man who sold me my car.

3 What's the name of the girl who is sharing a flat with Jane?

4 Jane's flatmate is the girl who my brother was going out with last year.

5 My first flat, which didn't even have a bathroom, was in the basement of an old house.

6 The landlord of my first flat, who owned all the flats in the building, was really mean.

C Write questions with a relative clause.

You were looking for a book the other day. Is this the one?
Is this the book *you were looking for?*

1 I saw you talking to a woman at the bus stop. Who was it?

What's the name of the woman ....

2 You wrote to ten hotels, didn't you? Have you had any replies?

Have you heard from any of the hotels ....

3 Tom grew up in an old farmhouse. Is it still there?

What has happened to the old farmhouse ....

4 Karin applied for a job last month. Did she get it?

Did Karin get the job ....

5 How about going out for dinner? Jack told us about a good restaurant last week.

How about going to the restaurant ....

D Translate the following sentences. Be careful with the commas!

1 Frau Fuchs, die unsere Blumen immer gießt (*water*), wenn wir im Urlaub sind, zieht um.
2 Die Freundin, auf die ich gestern gewartet habe, hatte einen Unfall.
3 David hat uns keine Postkarte geschrieben, was sehr ungewöhnlich ist.
4 Mein Chef, der aus Brasilien stammt (*come*), hat gestern geheiratet.
5 Wie ist der Name des Hotels, in dem wir letztes Jahr gewohnt haben?

33 Conditional I
Bedingungssätze I

A: What time will you be back?

B: About 12. I'll phone ~~when~~ if I'm late.

A: OK. Say hello to James for me if you see him.

B: OK. I'll give him a kiss from you if he ~~will be~~ is there. OK?

A: Well, I'd rather give him a kiss myself.

B: ~~I tell~~ I'll tell him that if I see him.

Der Unterschied zwischen if und when = „wenn"

- In der Bedeutung „immer, wenn" / „jedes Mal, wenn" sind when und if austauschbar.

  When/If you heat ice, it turns to water. *Wenn man Eis erhitzt, wird es zu Wasser.*

- In der Bedeutung „falls" muss „wenn" durch if wiedergegeben werden.

  If (~~When~~) it rains today, I'll stay at home. *Wenn es heute regnet, bleibe ich zu Hause.*

  Vergleiche:

  If I see Jim, I'll show him this letter. *Wenn/Falls ich Jim sehe, zeige ich ihm diesen Brief.*

  When I see Jim, I'll show him this letter. *Wenn/Sobald ich Jim sehe, zeige ich ihm diesen Brief.*

Bedingungssätze Typ I

- In Bedingungssätzen wird gesagt, was unter bestimmten Voraussetzungen geschieht bzw. geschehen wird. Solche Sätze bestehen aus zwei Teilen.

if-Satz: nennt die Bedingung	Hauptsatz: nennt die Folge
If I have time after work,	I'll go shopping this evening.

  Wenn ich nach der Arbeit Zeit habe, gehe ich heute Abend einkaufen.

  Der if-Satz kann hinter dem Hauptsatz stehen. In diesem Fall steht kein Komma dazwischen.

  Tom will phone if he needs our help. *Tom ruft an, wenn er unsere Hilfe braucht.*

- Im Bedingungssatz ist die Zeitenfolge festgelegt.

if-Satz: Gegenwart	Hauptsatz: will
If Ann finds anything out,	she'll tell (~~she tells~~) us tomorrow.
Wenn Ann etwas herausfindet,	*sagt sie uns morgen Bescheid.*
If the weather is bad,	we'll probably come home early.
Wenn das Wetter schlecht ist,	*kommen wir wahrscheinlich früher heim.*

! Kein will im if-Satz: If I am (~~will be~~) late, I'll phone.

- Im Hauptsatz kann auch die Befehlsform oder ein Modalverb stehen (can, might, must usw.).

  If you hear the postman, tell me. *Wenn du den Briefträger hörst, sag es mir.*

  If it stops raining, we can play tennis. *Wenn es aufhört zu regnen, können wir Tennis spielen.*

  Auch im if-Satz kann ein Modalverb stehen: If you can't come, please phone.

- In beiden Teilen (if-Satz und Hauptsatz) steht die einfache Gegenwart, wenn if „immer, wenn" / „jedes Mal, wenn" bedeutet (vgl. Beispiel oben: If you heat ice, it turns to water).

Das Wichtigste in Kürze

- „wenn" im zeitlichen Sinne („sobald", „immer, wenn", „jedes Mal, wenn") = when
  „wenn" im Sinne von „falls" = if
- if-Satz: Gegenwartsform – Hauptsatz: will
- Kein ~~will~~ im if-Satz!

Weitere Informationen → Units 34-35

A One sentence has a mistake. Which sentence is correct?

a I'll phone you if I'm late. ✔
b I'll phone you when I'm late.

1 **a** If you will see Tom, will you give him my new address?
b If you see Tom, will you give him my new address?

2 **a** If the weather is bad, we won't be able to have a barbecue.
b When the weather is bad, we won't be able to have a barbecue.

3 **a** Jane is very upset if you won't invite her to your party.
b Jane will be very upset if you don't invite her to your party.

4 **a** I won't be disappointed if you don't manage to come next weekend.
b I'm not disappointed if you won't manage to come next weekend.

B Make complete sentences with if.

If I / have to work late this evening, I / phone you.
If I have to work late this evening, I'll phone you.

1 If the taxi / not come soon, we / miss our train. ....

2 I'm sure you / feel better if you / lie down. ....

3 What / you / do if your boss / not let you take time off? ....

4 If I / not get to the bank today, I / change some money at the airport. ....

5 If you / get Sarah's birthday present, I / get the flowers for her. ....

6 I / give you a lift tomorrow if your car / still be at the garage. ....

C Complete these dialogues.

A: How are we getting to the station?
B: By taxi. If we *take* (take) the bus, we'*ll be* (be) late.

1 A: How are you going to get to Bill's party?
B: Well, if I .... (drive), I .... (not be able to) drink.

2 A: Are you going to post Carol's birthday card today?
B: No. It .... (still get) there on time if I .... (post) it tomorrow.

3 A: Is Sam's new girlfriend coming to your dinner party?
B: Yes. If I .... (not invite) her, he .... (not come).

4 A: Are you going to buy your children a pet?
B: I don't know. If I .... (buy) them one, I .... (probably have to) look after it.

5 A: The windows are very dirty.
B: Yes, but if I .... (clean) them, it .... (probably rain).

D Translate the following sentences.

1 Wenn er nicht bald kommt, fangen wir ohne ihn an.
2 Was machst du, wenn es am Wochenende regnet?
3 Gehst du morgen früher nachhause, wenn dein Chef dich lässt?
4 Ich kaufe den Mantel nicht, wenn er nicht reduziert ist.
5 Wenn Tim das Spiel morgen nicht gewinnt, wird er sehr enttäuscht sein.

34 Conditional II
Bedingungssätze II

A: What are your plans for today? What would you like to do?

B: Well, we could go and see that new film at the cinema if I ~~wouldn't~~ didn't have to go shopping.

A: We can go to the cinema later. How much shopping have you got? Can I help?

B: If I were you, I ~~didn't~~ wouldn't ask that.

A: Why?

B: I have to buy presents, and I hate it. Christmas ~~were~~ would be great if people didn't give presents.

„Was wäre, wenn ...“

- **In den folgenden if-Sätzen des Typs I wird eine Situation beschrieben, die durchaus möglich ist.**
  If it snows after Christmas, I'll go skiing. *Wenn es nach Weihnachten schneit, ...*
  If I have enough money, I'll go to the USA next summer. *Wenn ich genug Geld habe, ...*
  Der Sprecher sieht es als vorstellbar, vielleicht sogar wahrscheinlich an, dass es nach Weihnachten schneit bzw. dass er genug Geld hat.

- **Die folgenden if-Sätze beschreiben eine Situation, die unwahrscheinlich oder sogar unmöglich ist.**
  If it snowed in the Sahara, you could go skiing there.
  Wenn es in der Sahara schneite, könnte man dort Ski fahren.
  If I was/were rich, I'd have one house here and another in the USA.
  Wenn ich reich wäre, würde ich ein Haus hier und eins in den USA haben.
  Der Sprecher hält es für unwahrscheinlich oder unmöglich, dass es in der Sahara schneit bzw. dass er jemals reich wird. Er phantasiert, stellt sich vor, was in dem Fall wäre. Diese Art von Bedingungssatz wird als Typ II bezeichnet.

Bedingungssätze Typ II

- **Die Zeitenfolge in dieser Art von Bedingungssatz ist festgelegt.**

if-Satz: einfache Vergangenheit	Hauptsatz: would/could/might + Infinitiv
If I knew the answer,	I'd (= I would) tell you.
Wenn ich die Antwort wüsste,	*würde ich sie dir sagen.*
If it cost less,	I would buy it straightaway.
Wenn es weniger kostete,	*würde ich es sofort kaufen.*
If we lived in Australia,	we could spend Christmas on the beach.
Wenn wir in Australien lebten,	*könnten wir Weihnachten am Strand verbringen.*
If we asked Tony,	he might have an idea.
Wenn wir Tony fragen würden,	*könnte er vielleicht eine Idee haben.*

Im if-Satz steht die Vergangenheitsform – der Satz bezieht sich aber auf die Gegenwart/Zukunft.

! **Kein ~~would~~ im if-Satz: If I won (~~would win~~) a million dollars, I'd travel round the world.**

- **If I were you entspricht „an deiner/eurer/Ihrer Stelle“.**
  If I were you, I'd book early. *An deiner Stelle würde ich frühzeitig buchen.*
  I wouldn't wait if I were you. *An eurer Stelle würde ich nicht warten.*

Das Wichtigste in Kürze

- if-Satz: einfache Vergangenheit – Hauptsatz: would/could/might + Infinitiv
- Kein ~~would~~ im if-Satz!

Weitere Informationen → Unit 35

A One sentence has a mistake. Which sentence is correct?

a I would help you if I had more time. ✔
b I would help you if I would have more time.

1 a What did you do if you would lose your job?
b What would you do if you lost your job?

2 a If we would invite Paul to our wedding, he wouldn't come.
b If we invited Paul to our wedding, he wouldn't come.

3 a If I were you, I wouldn't buy that sofa.
b If I were you, I didn't buy that sofa.

4 a When I had more money, I would work part-time.
b If I had more money, I would work part-time.

B Make complete sentences with if.

The grass is really wet. If I / be you, I / not cut it today.
If I were you, I wouldn't cut it today.

1 Why do you work so hard? If you / work less, you / have more time for your family.

2 I don't understand why Sue spends so much money on clothes. If she / not buy so many, she / be able to afford more holidays.

3 Have you seen this job ad? It sounds really interesting. If I / be you, I / apply for it.

4 Jim's often late for work. If he / be more punctual, he / probably get on better with his boss.

5 Why are they going to Spain in February? If they / wait a couple of months, it / not be so cold.

C Make complete sentences. Use conditional I or II.

If I / feel better at the weekend, I / go for a walk.
If I feel better at the weekend, I'll go for a walk.

If I / win on the lottery, I / travel round the world.
If I won on the lottery, I would travel round the world.

1 I'm sure it will never happen, but if I / lose my passport, I / go to the police.

2 You love ballet, don't you? If you / want to come with us on Saturday, I / try to get another ticket.

3 If I / be you, I / save some money every month.

4 If I / not have time to call you this evening, I / phone you tomorrow – I promise.

5 We always have to find someone to look after our dog when we're away. If we / not have one, I'm sure we / go on holiday more often.

6 Don't book a taxi. I / give you a lift to the airport tomorrow if your husband can't take you.

D Translate the following sentences.

1 An Ihrer Stelle würde ich nicht am Freitag fahren.
2 Ich würde dir helfen, wenn ich am Wochenende hier wäre.
3 Wenn ich nicht zweimal umsteigen müsste, würde ich mit dem Bus zur Arbeit fahren.
4 Meine Schwester würde nur Teilzeit arbeiten, wenn sie nicht das Geld brauchte.
5 Wenn meine Eltern nicht so weit weg wohnten, würde ich sie öfter besuchen.

35 Conditional III
Bedingungssätze III

A: Oh damn, no coffee! I used the last of it last night.

B: I've just been shopping. If you ~~would have told~~ *had told* me, I could have bought some.

A: Sorry. My memory is getting really bad.

B: You ~~could do~~ *could have done* something about it last year if you ~~went~~ *had gone* on that memory training course with me.

A: What course was that?

B: See? You've forgotten. You ~~had missed~~ *would have missed* Dave's party last Saturday if I hadn't reminded you.

„Was wäre damals gewesen, wenn ..."

- **In den folgenden if-Sätzen wird eine vergangene Situation beschrieben, die sich nicht so ereignet hat.**

  If I had gone to Spain for my holiday, I would have had good weather.
  Wenn ich nach Spanien in Urlaub gefahren wäre, hätte ich gutes Wetter gehabt.
  Realität: Ich bin nicht nach Spanien gefahren.

  If we had had enough money, we would have bought the car.
  Wenn wir genug Geld gehabt hätten, hätten wir das Auto gekauft.
  Realität: Wir hatten nicht genug Geld.

  Die beschriebene Situation war nie Wirklichkeit und kann es auch nicht werden, weil sie der abgeschlossenen Vergangenheit angehört. Der Sprecher stellt sich aber vor, was gewesen wäre. Diese Art von Bedingungssatz wird als Typ III bezeichnet.

Bedingungssätze Typ III

- **Auch in Bedingungssätzen des Typs III ist die Zeitenfolge festgelegt.**

if-Satz: Past Perfect	Hauptsatz: would/could/might + have + Partizip Perfekt
If I had seen Ann,	I would have asked her for the address.
Wenn ich Ann gesehen hätte,	*hätte ich sie um die Adresse gebeten.*
If I had driven more slowly,	I could have avoided the accident.
Wenn ich langsamer gefahren wäre,	*hätte ich den Unfall vermeiden können.*
If we had asked Tony,	he might have helped us.
Wenn wir Tony gefragt hätten,	*hätte er uns vielleicht geholfen.*

- **Oft werden verneinte Formen gebraucht.**

  I wouldn't have dropped the plate if it hadn't been so hot.
  Ich hätte den Teller nicht fallen lassen, wenn er nicht so heiß gewesen wäre.
  If I had seen the colours in daylight, I wouldn't have bought this sofa.
  Wenn ich die Farben bei Tageslicht gesehen hätte, hätte ich dieses Sofa nicht gekauft.

Das Wichtigste in Kürze

- if-Satz: Past Perfect – Hauptsatz: would/could/might + have + Partizip Perfekt

A One sentence has a mistake. Which sentence is correct?

a If we would have bought our car last year, it had been cheaper.
b If we had bought our car last year, it would have been cheaper. ✔

1 **a** If I'd taken my camera on holiday, I could have taken some photos.
b If I would have taken my camera on holiday, I could have taken some photos.

2 **a** I wouldn't have been late for work if I didn't forget to set my alarm clock.
b I wouldn't have been late for work if I hadn't forgotten to set my alarm clock.

3 **a** Were you able to buy your flat if your uncle hadn't left you some money?
b Would you have been able to buy your flat if your uncle hadn't left you some money?

4 **a** If there hadn't been so many interruptions, I might have finished this work yesterday.
b If there weren't so many interruptions, I would finish this work yesterday.

B Make complete sentences with if.

Dave lost his wallet on holiday. If someone / not find it in the street, he / not get it back.
If someone hadn't found it in the street, he wouldn't have got it back.

1 We went to Spain last week. If we / not manage to get a last-minute holiday, we / not be able to go away.

....

2 I don't know why you didn't apply for that job last month. I'm sure you / get it if you / apply.

....

3 The management didn't increase their offer. The workers / not go on strike if the management / agree to pay them more.

....

4 Gary failed his final exams. If he / study harder, he / might pass.

....

5 Jane had no idea about the company's financial problems when she accepted a job there. She / take the job if she / know?

....

C Write sentences with if.

Paul went on a training course last year and met Jane.
If Paul hadn't gone on the training course, he wouldn't have met Jane.

1 I didn't listen to the radio in the morning so I didn't know about the hold-up on the motorway.

....

2 Sarah didn't apply for a visa early enough and so she had to cancel her trip to Australia.

....

3 We didn't have our mobile phone with us, so we couldn't phone to say we'd be late.

....

4 I took a risk and invested all my money in some shares. A year later I made a lot of money on them.

....

5 The children didn't know that the ice on the lake was too thin and they went skating.

....

D Translate the following sentences.

1 Wenn ich nicht so viel Gepäck gehabt hätte, wäre ich mit dem Bus und nicht mit einem Taxi gekommen.
2 Wenn wir gewusst hätten, wie voll die Ausstellung (*exhibition*) am Wochenende ist, hätten wir bis Montag gewartet.
3 Wenn du mich nicht angerufen hättest, hätte ich verschlafen. (verschlafen = *oversleep*)
4 Der Unfall wäre nicht passiert, wenn Pete nicht so viel getrunken hätte.
5 Wären Sie umgezogen, wenn Sie gewusst hätten, wie laut es in dieser Straße ist?

36 Indirect speech (1)
Indirekte Rede (1)

A: Have you heard this crazy story about Dave?

B: Yes. Jim told me. He ~~told that~~ *said that / told me that* Dave ate a fish and found a gold ring in it.

A: Do you believe it? Which restaurant was this? Who else was there?

B: Well, Jim ~~said~~ *told* me that Ann was there.

A: What does she say? Has anyone spoken to her?

B: I haven't, and when I saw Jim yesterday afternoon, he said that he ~~hasn't~~ *hadn't* spoken to her either.

Direkte Rede – Indirekte Rede

- **Was jemand sagt, kann man direkt (wörtlich, als Zitat) wiedergeben oder indirekt „berichten".**

  Direkte Rede: Ann said, **"Tom is an idiot."** *Ann sagte: „Tom ist ein Idiot".*

  Indirekte Rede: Ann said **that Tom was an idiot**. *Ann sagte, Tom sei/wäre ein Idiot.*

  Auch Gedanken kann man „berichten".

  Gedanke: "Sally will be late." → **Bericht:** I thought/knew **that Sally would be late**.

! **Die indirekte Rede leitet man meist mit say oder tell ein. Nach tell nennt man die Person, der etwas gesagt wurde. Wird die Person nicht genannt, so muss say verwendet werden.**

He **told me** (~~told~~) that he knows London well. *Er sagte mir, dass er London gut kenne.*

He **said** (~~said me~~) that he knows London well.

! **Vor that darf kein Komma stehen – that wird aber oft auch weggelassen.**

Tony **said that** (~~said, that~~) he will be here at six. Ann **said she** (~~said, she~~) loves fish.

Zeitverschiebung in der indirekten Rede

- **Steht das einleitende Verb der indirekten Rede in der Vergangenheit (z.B. said), so wird das Verb des berichteten Satzes oft um eine Zeitstufe in die Vergangenheit „verschoben".**

Gegenwart → Vergangenheit	"I **feel** ill."	→	She said (that) she **felt** ill.
	"I'**m working**."	→	She said (that) she **was working**.
Present Perfect → Past Perfect	"I'**ve had** a dream."	→	She said (that) she **had had** a dream.
can/may → **could/might**	"I **can/may** come."	→	She said (that) she **could/might** come.
will → **would**	"I'**ll** be there."	→	She said (that) she **would** be there.

- **Zeitstufen der Vergangenheit (außer Present Perfect) sowie die Modalverben could (= *könnte*), might, should, would bleiben fast alle unverändert.**

Vergangenheit	"We **saw** Tom there."	→	She said they **saw** (oder: **had seen**) Tom there.
	"He **was smoking**."	→	She said he **was** (oder: **had been**) **smoking**.
Past Perfect	"I **had eaten**."	→	She said she **had eaten**.
could/might/should	"I **could** help."	→	She said she **could** help.
would	"I **wouldn't** tell him."	→	She said she **wouldn't** tell him.

- **Eine Zeitverschiebung muss nicht stattfinden, wenn das Berichtete immer oder immer noch gilt.**

  "When I **see** him, I'**ll ask** him." → She said she'**ll ask** him when she **sees** him. He'll be here soon.

  Man wählt aber bewusst die Zeitverschiebung, wenn man sich von dem, was man berichtet, distanzieren will und zeigen will, dass man dessen Wahrheitsgehalt nicht garantiert.

  Politiker: "Inflation is low." → **Zeitungsbericht: The government said that inflation was low.**

Das Wichtigste in Kürze

- **Zeitverschiebung bei einleitendem Verb in der Vergangenheit: Gegenwart → Vergangenheit, Present Perfect → Past Perfect, can → could, may → might, will → would**

Weitere Informationen → Unit 37

A One sentence has a mistake. Which sentence is correct?

a "I'm hungry." ⇢ Sue said me she was hungry.
b "I'm hungry." ⇢ Sue said she was hungry. ✔

1 a Tom told me he had seen Spielberg's latest film.
b Tom told he had seen Spielberg's latest film.

2 a Jane said me she had had a good holiday.
b Jane said she had had a good holiday.

3 a The teacher told us, that 32°F is 0°C.
b The teacher told us that 32°F is 0°C.

4 a Al told us an hour ago that Ann has phoned.
b Al told us an hour ago that Ann had phoned.

5 a "I'm meeting Jo." ⇢ Ed said he met Jo.
b "I'm meeting Jo." ⇢ Ed said he was meeting Jo.

6 a "I want to go." ⇢ She said she would go.
b "I want to go." ⇢ She said she wanted to go.

B Put the following sentences into indirect speech.

"I don't want to go to Spain again." ⇢ Sandra explained that *she didn't want to go to Spain again.*

1 "I can help at the weekend and Sue may have time too." ⇢ Paul's awful. Two weeks ago he promised he .... and said Sue .... and then neither of them came!
2 "We've bought a house in the country. We think it will be better for the children." ⇢ When I last saw Mrs Adams she told me they ....
3 "You'll have to work harder if you want to pass the exam." ⇢ The teacher told me I .... In fact I passed without any problems!
4 "I've had two job interviews but I'm not really interested in either of the jobs." ⇢ Tom said he .... So he's still looking.

C Report the following things which you read in the newspaper and don't really believe.

1 "Petrol will soon be much cheaper." ⇢ A government spokesperson promised that
....
2 "Temperatures in June were lower than in March." ⇢ The weather report claimed that
....
3 "Bill Gates has decided to give all his money to charity." ⇢ A report in last week's paper said that
....
4 "Prince Charles is getting married again." ⇢ The headline in yesterday's paper said that
....
5 "Scientists have found a cure for Aids." ⇢ An article in last Saturday's paper claimed that
....

D Complete these sentences using the information in brackets.

A: I'll be in Hamburg on Wednesday.
B: Last week you told me (Thursday) *you'd be in Hamburg on Thursday.*

1 A: I'm hungry. Let's go out for dinner.
B: Half an hour ago you said (not hungry / not want to go out for dinner) ....
....
2 A: I'm going to apply for this job.
B: When I told you about the job last week, you said (not interested in it) ....
....
3 A: I think I'll get red wine for the party.
B: Last week you said (white wine) ....
4 A: I can't come round this evening because my car is at the garage.
B: You've never got time! Yesterday you said you (can't come) ....
because you (have to work) ....

37 Indirect speech (2)
Indirekte Rede (2)

A: Who was that I saw you with last Tuesday?

B: Celia Burns. She said she had seen you ~~yesterday~~ the day before.

A: You mean last Monday. Where?

B: In the Green Chopsticks. She asked who ~~were you~~ you were.

A: So what did you say? I think I'd like to meet her.

B: Well that's good, because I asked her if she ~~did want~~ wanted to meet you.

Fragen in der indirekten Rede

- Entscheidungsfragen leitet man mit ask + if/whether (= *ob*) ein. Nach ask steht kein Komma. Die Zeiten der direkten Rede werden „verschoben" wie in Aussagesätzen (s. Unit 36).
  "Is it raining?" → He asked if/whether it was raining. *Er fragte, ob es regnete.*
  "Can you swim?" → He asked if/whether I could swim. *Er fragte, ob ich schwimmen könn(t)e.*

  do/does/did erscheint in der indirekten Frage nicht.
  "Do you know Dave?" → He asked if/whether I knew Dave.
  "Did Ann go to the party?" → He asked if/whether Ann went to the party.

- wh-Fragen leitet man mit ask + Fragewort ein.
  "Where's Tom?" → He asked where Tom was.
  "Who have you spoken to?" → He asked who I had spoken to.

- Auch Ausdrücke wie want to know / find out, wonder können die indirekte Rede einleiten.
  "Who's talking?" → He wanted to know / wanted to find out / wondered who was talking.

Bitten und Befehle in der indirekten Rede

- Bitten gibt man mit ask somebody (not) to do something wieder.
  "I'd like some help, please." → He asked me to help him. *Er bat mich, ihm zu helfen.*
  "Please don't smoke." → He asked me not to smoke. *Er bat mich, nicht zu rauchen.*

- Befehle gibt man mit tell somebody (not) to do something wieder.
  "Go home." → He told me to go home. *Er sagte mir, dass ich nachhause gehen sollte.*
  "Don't wait." → He told me not to wait. *Er sagte mir, dass ich nicht warten sollte.*

Orts- und Zeitbestimmungen in der indirekten Rede

! Berichtet man etwas an einem anderen Ort bzw. nachdem ein bestimmter Zeitraum vorbei ist, so muss man bestimmte Orts- und Zeitbestimmungen der direkten Rede anders wiedergeben.

"Tom's not here." → He said Tom wasn't there.
"I can't come today." → He said he couldn't come that day.
"I met Bill yesterday." → He said he had met Bill the day before.
"We're leaving tomorrow." → He said they were leaving the next day.
"It's my 30th birthday this week/month/year." → He said it was ... that week/month/year.
"Ed died last Sunday/week/month/year." → He said Ed had died the Sunday/week/... before.
"She's moving next Monday/week/month/year." → He said ... the following Monday/week/... .

Das Wichtigste in Kürze

- Indirekte Fragen: ask + if/whether, ask + Fragewort
- Indirekte Bitten/Befehle: ask/tell somebody (not) to do something
- here → there; today → that day; yesterday → the day before; tomorrow → the next day; this ... → that ... ; last ... → the ... before; next ... → the following ...

A One sentence has a mistake. Which sentence is correct?

a Tom asked me if I did know how old Sandra was.
b Tom asked me if I knew how old Sandra was. ✓

1 a The teacher asked the children where their homework was.
b The teacher asked the children where was their homework.

2 a "Is Sue coming?" → Jane asked me, if Sue was coming.
b "Is Sue coming?" → Jane asked me if Sue was coming.

3 a "We moved yesterday." → Ann wrote and told us they'd moved the day before.
b "We moved yesterday." → Ann wrote and told us they'd moved yesterday.

4 a "Can you come a bit earlier?" → Dave asked us to come a bit earlier.
b "Can you come a bit earlier?" → Dave said us to come a bit earlier.

B Report the following requests and commands.

"Please don't be late." (Paul/us) *Paul asked us not to be late.*
"Be quiet!" (teacher/children) *The teacher told the children to be quiet.*

1 "Drive more slowly!" (driving instructor / student) ....
2 "Stay in bed and don't smoke." (doctor/patient) ....
3 "Can you help me, please?" (old lady / man) ....
4 "Don't forget your passports." (guide/tourists) ....
5 "Could you finish the report?" (boss/secretary) ....

C Report these sentences.

Sue: "We are getting married next week."
Sue wrote and told us that *they were getting married the following week.*

1 Jane: "My husband is starting a new job today."
I spoke to Jane a week ago and she said ....
2 Ed: "We're meeting in the Red Lion next week."
Ed rang Tom and told him .... but he didn't make it.
3 Carol: "Sue will be here soon – she's not normally late."
Carol said Sue .... and then her husband rang to say she'd had an accident.
4 Ann: "We moved yesterday. As soon as we have a new phone number, I'll let you know."
I saw Ann a month ago and she told me ....
....

D Report these questions.

1 John: "Did you get a birthday card from Sue?"
John asked me ....
2 Jane: "Do you know what time the concert starts?"
Jane asked me .... and then she was still late!
3 Mary: "Can you babysit for us next Saturday?"
Two weeks ago Mary asked me ....
I said 'yes' and then I forgot.
4 Tom: "Where are we meeting the others this evening?"
It's funny. On Saturday Tom asked me ....
and then he didn't come.
5 Dave: "Could I borrow your bike next weekend?"
Four weeks ago Dave asked me ....
and he still hasn't brought it back.

38 Reflexive pronouns and verbs
Reflexivpronomen und -verben

A: ~~Help you~~ Help yourself to another drink.
B: Thanks, but I think it's time for me to go.
A: Oh, that's a pity. We must ~~meet us~~ meet again soon.
B: Yes, that would be nice. Have you been invited to the opening of Donald Webster's exhibition?
A: No, we don't know ~~us~~ each other very well.
B: He's very good. Would you like to go? You could come with me, if you like.

Formen

Einzahl:	-self	myself	yourself	himself, herself, itself
		mir/mich selbst	*dir/dich/[Sie] sich selbst*	*sich selbst*
Mehrzahl:	-selves	ourselves	yourselves	themselves
		uns selbst	*euch/[Sie] sich selbst*	*sich selbst*

Gebrauch im Rückbezug auf das Subjekt

- Im Englischen verwendet man im Rückbezug auf das Subjekt keine Personalpronomen.
  We saw ourselves (~~us~~) on a big screen. *Wir sahen uns auf einem großen Bildschirm.*
  I taught myself (~~me~~) chess. *Ich habe mir selbst Schach beigebracht.*
  She can take care of herself. *Sie kann auf sich aufpassen.*
  There are the drinks. Help yourselves, and enjoy yourselves! … *Bedient euch, und viel Spaß!*

  Ausnahme: nach Präpositionen des Ortes (in front of, behind, with usw.)
  Tom heard a noise behind him (~~himself~~). … *hinter sich.* He had a lot of money with him. … *bei sich.*

! each other entspricht „uns/euch/sich" im Sinne von „uns/euch/sich gegenseitig".
We write each other (~~us~~) e-mails. *Wir schreiben uns (gegenseitig) E-Mails.*
After 20 years of marriage they know each other (~~them~~) very well. … *kennen sie sich sehr gut.*

! Deutsche Reflexivverben entsprechen nicht immer Reflexivverben im Englischen.
We can't afford that. *Wir können uns das nicht leisten.*
When will he decide? *Wann entscheidet er sich?*

afford *sich leisten*
change *sich umziehen*
complain *sich beschweren*
concentrate *sich konzentrieren*
feel *sich fühlen*
imagine *sich vorstellen*
lie down *sich hinlegen*
meet *sich treffen*
relax *sich ausruhen/sich entspannen*
remember *sich erinnern*
sit down *sich setzen*
wonder *sich fragen*
worry *sich Sorgen machen*

wash, dress/undress sind nur dann reflexiv, wenn die Tätigkeit Anstrengungen erfordert.
Little Tim is only two. He can't dress himself yet. Ed's broken his arm. He can't wash himself.

Gebrauch zur Hervorhebung = deutsch „selbst/selber"

- Reflexivpronomen dienen auch zur Hervorhebung. Sie entsprechen dann „selbst/selber".
  We designed the house ourselves. *Wir haben das Haus selbst entworfen.*
  The teacher didn't know the answer to question 5 himself. … *wusste die Antwort … selber nicht.*

Das Wichtigste in Kürze

- Einzahl: -self — Mehrzahl: -selves
- „uns/euch/sich gegenseitig" = each other
- Wichtige deutsche Reflexivverben sind keine Reflexivverben im Englischen:
  sich fühlen, sich konzentrieren, sich vorstellen, sich treffen, sich Sorgen machen usw.

A One sentence has a mistake. Which sentence is correct?

a Be careful with that knife or you'll cut yourself! ✔
b Be careful with that knife or you'll cut you!

1 **a** When are we meeting us?
b When are we meeting?

2 **a** Be quiet! I can't concentrate myself.
b Be quiet! I can't concentrate.

3 **a** I remember me meeting you at Sue's party.
b I remember meeting you at Sue's party.

4 **a** How long have we known each other now?
b How long have we known us now?

5 **a** I paid for myself.
b I paid for me.

6 **a** Help you to some more food.
b Help yourself to some more food.

B Complete these sentences with the translation of the verbs in brackets.

(sich sorgen für) My grandmother can no longer look after herself.

1 (sich fühlen) Sue .... much better today.

2 (sich fragen) I .... if Tom will phone.

3 (sich vorstellen) I can't .... why you don't want to go.

4 (sich amüsieren) We really .... at the party last week.

5 (sich verletzen) Gary fell off the ladder and ....

6 (sich konzentrieren) It was hot and the students couldn't ....

C If necessary, add the correct reflexive pronouns or each other.

The students recorded their role play and then watched themselves on video.
The students always speak to each other in English in the class.

1 You shouldn't blame .... for the accident. It was the other driver's fault.

2 What time are we meeting .... ?

3 David is very selfish – he only thinks about ....

4 Sue and Dave are so different but they really seem to like ....

5 Relax .... and make .... at home.

Help .... if you would like something to drink.

6 I can't afford .... to visit Jane but we haven't seen ....

for so long and she will only worry .... if I don't go.

D Translate the following sentences.

1 Ich frage mich, wann wir ankommen werden.
2 Gestern hat Paul sich beschwert – er konnte sich nicht konzentrieren, weil die Nachbarn so laut waren.
3 Wir treffen uns um acht, aber ich kann mich nicht erinnern, wo.
4 Ich habe viele Fotos von meinen Kindern, aber keins (*none*) von mir selbst.
5 Am Wochenende lege ich mich gerne hin und entspanne mich.

39 Adjectives – Adverbs
Adjektive – Adverbien

A: A great party, isn't it?

B: Yes, Tom and Ann are so ~~good~~ well organized and Tom cooks so ~~beautiful.~~ beautifully

A: Mm. Have you tried this pie here?

B: I can't see very ~~good~~ well without my glasses. Wait a moment. Oh, that's better. Yes, it looks ~~well.~~ good

A: It tastes wonderful, too.

B: They've really worked ~~hardly,~~ hard haven't they?

Adjektive

- Adjektive beschreiben, wie jemand/etwas ist. Sie beziehen sich auf ein Nomen oder Pronomen. Sie stehen vor einem Nomen (1) oder nach be (2).

1 Sue is a careful ***driver***.
... eine vorsichtige Fahrerin.

2 ***Sue/She*** is careful.
... ist vorsichtig.

Adverbien

- Adverbien beschreiben, wie etwas geschieht, und beziehen sich auf ein Verb (1). Sie können aber auch ein anderes Wort verstärken oder abschwächen. Dann beziehen sie sich auf ein Adjektiv (2), auf ein anderes Adverb (3) oder auf ein Partizip (4).

1 Sue ***drives*** carefully.
... fährt vorsichtig.

2 She is especially ***careful*** in fog.
... besonders vorsichtig.

3 She doesn't drive particularly ***slowly***.
... besonders langsam.

4 And she's always so well ***prepared*** on a long trip, too.
... gut vorbereitet.

Form von Adverbien

- Meist hängt man -ly an das Adjektiv: David is a slow reader. He reads slowly. Schreibbesonderheiten wie easy – easily; terrible – terribly; automatic – automatically siehe Seite 111.

- Einige wenige Adverbien haben die gleiche Form wie das Adjektiv: early *(früh)*, late *(spät)*, fast *(schnell)*, hard *(hart, schwer, heftig, kräftig)*.

Verwechslungsgefahr: It rained hard. *Es regnete heftig.* — It hardly rained. *Es regnete kaum.*
Ed came late. *Ed kam zu spät.* — Have you seen him lately? *... in der letzten Zeit?*

! Sonderfall good (Adjektiv) – well (Adverb): She's a good player. She plays well.

Adjektiv statt Adverb nach bestimmten Verben

! Auf bestimmte Verben folgt ein Adjektiv, kein Adverb. Das Bezugswort ist ein Nomen oder Pronomen, nicht ein Verb. Es wird gesagt, wie jemand/etwas ist.

– Verben, die einen Zustand beschreiben: be *(sein)*, seem *(scheinen)*, become *(werden)*, stay/remain *(bleiben)*
– Verben, die eine Eigenschaft ausdrücken: look *(aussehen)*, sound *(klingen, sich anhören)*, feel *(sich fühlen, sich anfühlen)*, taste *(schmecken)*, smell *(riechen)*

He seemed/looked excited (~~excitedly~~). *Er erschien aufgeregt. / Er sah aufgeregt aus.*

Das Wichtigste in Kürze

- Ein Adjektiv sagt, wie jemand/etwas ist – Ein Adverb sagt, wie etwas geschieht
- Kein Adverb, sondern Adjektiv nach u.a. be, seem, look, sound, feel, smell

Weitere Informationen → Units 40-41

A One sentence has a mistake. Which sentence is correct?

a My colleague speaks English very well. ✔
b My colleague speaks English very good.

1 a I always feel tired. I work too hard.
b I always feel tired. I work too hardly.

2 a We're good prepared for our next meeting.
b We're well prepared for our next meeting.

3 a My sister doesn't seem very happily.
b My sister doesn't seem very happy.

4 a My boss is serious ill.
b My boss is seriously ill.

5 a Harry was hurt quite bad in the accident.
b Harry was hurt quite badly in the accident.

6 a We don't know our neighbours very well.
b We don't know our neighbours very good.

B Rewrite these sentences using an adverb instead of an adjective.

Your English is really **good**. You speak English really well.

1 David is an extremely **careful** driver. David drives ....
2 They are **good** dancers. They dance ....
3 She is a really **fast** runner. She runs ....
4 We have **regular** meetings. We meet ....
5 His death was completely **unexpected**. He died ....

C Complete these conversations with adjectives or adverbs.

1 A: Sorry I'm .... (late/lately) but we've been so busy .... (late/lately).
B: That's OK, but be .... (careful/carefully) – don't work too .... (hard/hardly).
A: I won't. I've been sleeping .... (bad/badly) – that's the .... (real/really) problem.
2 A: Hello, Jane! Did you have a .... (good/well) holiday?
B: Yes, thanks. The weather was .... (beautiful/beautifully) – it .... (hard/hardly) rained.
A: Really? That's .... (unusual/unusually) for England, isn't it?
3 A: What's the matter with Don? He looks so .... (unhappy/unhappily).
B: He's been .... (terrible/terribly) worried about losing his job since the management changed .... (sudden/suddenly) last month.
A: Oh dear, and his wife's job isn't very .... (good/well) paid either, is it?
4 A: I've just heard the .... (terrible/terribly) news about your sister's accident. Was she .... (bad/badly) injured?
B: No, thank goodness. She was only .... (slight/slightly) hurt, but her boyfriend's injuries are more .... (serious/seriously).
A: There have been so many .... (bad/badly) accidents on that part of the road. It's really .... (dangerous/dangerously).
5 A: I feel so .... (angry/angrily). Our new neighbours are really .... (noisy/noisily). Their music is always so .... (loud/loudly) – I just can't concentrate on my work .... (proper/properly).
B: Why don't you ask them .... (nice/nicely) to turn it down?
A: I did last week and since then they've had two .... (noisy/noisily) parties which finished really .... (late/lately)!

D Translate the following sentences.

1 John fühlte sich fürchterlich. Er war fürchterlich müde.
2 Gewöhnlich träumt er nicht viel. Eines Abends hatte er einen ungewöhnlichen Traum.
3 Plötzlich hörte er etwas. Ein plötzliches Geräusch weckte ihn auf.
4 Sein Sohn und seine Freunde hörten laute Musik und redeten laut im Wohnzimmer.
5 „Du siehst sehr böse aus," sagte sein Sohn. „Warum siehst du mich so böse an?"

40 Comparison of adjectives and adverbs
Steigerung von Adjektiven und Adverbien

A: I'd like to go by train. It's more comfortable.

B: Yes, but it's ~~much more cheaper~~ *much cheaper* by bus.

A: True, but on a train I can get up and walk about. If you're as tall as me, bus seats are murder.

B: Well, shall we fly then? Flying is faster ~~as~~ *than* going by bus or train.

A: Yes, but the leg-room on charter planes is so small.

B: Is it? I thought the seats on a plane were the same ~~like~~ *as* on a train.

Steigerungsformen von Adjektiven und Adverbien

- Durch Anhängen von -er/-est werden gesteigert:
  – einsilbige Adjektive (Schreibbesonderheiten siehe Seite 111): tall – taller – (the) tallest

  – zweisilbige Adjektive auf -y (angry, dirty, easy, funny, happy, lovely, lucky usw.)
  Dabei wird y zu i: easy – easier – (the) easiest.

  – Adverbien, die mit einem Adjektiv formgleich sind (early, late, hard, fast, long):
  Who gets up early/earlier/(the) earliest? *Wer steht früh/früher/am frühesten auf?*

- Durch Voranstellen von more/most werden gesteigert:
  – mehrsilbige Adjektive (außer zweisilbige auf -y): careful – more careful – (the) most careful

  – -ly-Adverbien: Ed works carefully / more carefully / most carefully.
  Anstelle von more/most quickly, slowly, loudly werden jedoch oft Formen mit -er/-est gebraucht.
  Ed worked slower / (the) slowest. Who sang louder / (the) loudest?

- Ausnahmen und Sonderformen
  good/well – better – (the) best *gut – besser – (der/die/das) beste / am besten*
  much – more – most *viel – mehr – am meisten*
  bad(ly) – worse – (the) worst *schlecht – schlechter – (der/die/das) schlechteste / am schlechtesten*
  little – less – least *wenig – weniger – am wenigsten*
  far – further – furthest *weit – weiter – (der/die/das) weiteste / am weitesten*

Vergleiche:

- Setzt man zwei Personen/Dinge gleich, wird der Vergleichssatz mit as gebildet.
  I'm as careful as Phil. I drive as carefully as Phil. ... *so vorsichtig wie Phil.*
  I'm not as careful as Ann. I don't drive as carefully as Ann. ... *nicht so vorsichtig wie Ann.*

  Auch nach the same steht as: Your coat is the same colour as (~~like~~) mine.

! Nach Adjektiven und Adverbien in der ersten Steigerungsstufe wird nicht as, sondern than gebraucht.
Dave is taller than (~~as~~) his sister. *Dave ist größer als seine Schwester.*
The book is more exciting than (~~as~~) the film. *Das Buch ist spannender als der Film.*
It all happened sooner than (~~as~~) expected. *Es geschah alles schneller als erwartet.*
Sonia sings much better than (~~much more better as~~) Angela. *Sonia singt viel besser als Angela.*

- Nach as bzw. than stehen alleinstehende Personalpronomen in der Objektform.
  Don isn't as tall as me. But I'm older than him. ... *nicht so groß wie ich ... älter als er.*

Das Wichtigste in Kürze

- Steigerung: Kurze Adjektive: -er/-est. Längere Adjektive und -ly-Adverbien: more/most
- Vergleiche: Bei Gleichsetzung: as. Nach der ersten Steigerungsstufe: than

A One sentence has a mistake. Which sentence is correct?

a This exercise is easyer than the last one.
b This exercise is easier than the last one. ✔

1 a She's the most important person in the firm.
b She's the importantest person in the firm.

2 a He speaks English much better than me.
b He speaks English much more better than me.

3 a I do more work as my colleague.
b I do more work than my colleague.

4 a He arrived so early as I did.
b He arrived as early as I did.

5 a This coat is cheaper than that one.
b This coat is more cheap than that one.

6 a I've made the same mistakes like you.
b I've made the same mistakes as you.

B Make comparisons and add as or than if necessary.

This film is *more interesting* (interesting) *than* the film we saw last week.

1 It's much .... (hard) to find a job today .... it was ten years ago.

2 A glass of water in this restaurant costs the same .... a glass of wine. Normally wine is .... (expensive) .... water.

3 It's much .... (difficult) to get a cheap flight to New York .... I had expected.

4 The blue pullover is the .... (cheap) of them all, but is it really the .... (good)?

5 I've just had some bad news. My grandmother's illness is .... (serious) .... the doctors first thought.

6 What's the .... (bad) thing that has ever happened to you?

C Make questions using comparatives.

Sorry. What did you say? Can you speak a bit *louder*, please?

1 This restaurant is too expensive. Can we go to a .... one?

2 You're speaking too fast. I don't understand. Could you speak ...., please?

3 This jacket is too small. Do you have a .... one, please?

4 Sue didn't seem very well when I last saw her. Is she .... now?

5 I'm sure you're always tired because you go to bed so late. Why don't you go a bit ....?

6 The questions in the first part of the test were easy. Were they easy in the second part, too, or were they ....?

D Translate the following sentences.

1 Die Fahrt (*journey*) nach Leeds ist lang, viel länger als ich dachte.
2 Du hast die gleiche Jacke wie ich.
3 Dieses Jahr wohnen (*stay*) wir in einem Hotel weiter weg vom Strand als letztes Jahr.
4 Meine Schwester und ich sind Zwillinge (*twins*), aber sie ist viel dünner als ich.
5 Letztes Jahr hatten wir die schlechteste Ernte (*harvest*) seit 1990.

41 Position of adverbs
Stellung der Adverbien

A: Which country do you like best?

B: I like ~~very much Italy~~ *Italy very much*.

A: How often do you go there?

B: We ~~go usually~~ *usually go* once a year, in the summer.

A: Are you going this year?

B: Yes, but we are going ~~this year later~~ *later this year*. In October.

Kategorien von Adverbien

- **Es gibt verschiedene Arten von Adverbien: zwei wurden bereits in Unit 39 vorgestellt.**

– **Adverbien der Zeit beantworten die Frage „wann?“:** Dave phoned yesterday.

– **Adverbien der Häufigkeit (always usw.) beantworten die Frage „wie oft?“:** It's never cold.

– **Adverbien der Art und Weise (oft mit -ly, siehe Unit 39) beantworten die Frage „wie?“:** I slept badly.

– **Adverbien des Ortes beantworten die Frage „wo(hin/her)?“:** London is north of here.

– **Gradadverbien (very usw., siehe Unit 39) beantworten die Frage „wie sehr/viel?“:** He's very old.

– **Satzadverbien beziehen sich auf eine gesamte Aussage:** Perhaps the weather will improve.

Stellung von Adverbien

- **Für ein Adverb gibt es grundsätzlich drei Stellungsmöglichkeiten: am Satzanfang, am Satzende, in der Satzmitte. Mit Satzmitte ist gemeint:**

– **vor einem Vollverb:** Don never *smokes*. (~~Don smokes never.~~)

– **hinter dem (ersten) Hilfsverb:** We *have* just *eaten* supper.

– **hinter dem Voll- oder Hilfsverb be:** Angela *is* always late. She *is* just *coming*.

! **Ein Adverb kann normalerweise nicht zwischen Verb und Objekt stehen.**
I never *smoke* cigars. (~~I smoke never cigars.~~) I *ate* fish yesterday. (~~I ate yesterday fish.~~)

- **Kurze Adverbien der Zeit (ever, just, now, soon, still und already) stehen meist in der Satzmitte, andere Adverbien der Zeit (today/yesterday/tomorrow, Angaben mit ago, Uhr- und Tageszeiten usw.) am Satzende.**
I'*m* still tired. I *worked* all last night. Ed *has* just *phoned*. He'*ll arrive* tomorrow.

- **Adverbien der Häufigkeit (always, usually, often, sometimes, rarely, never) stehen meist in der Satzmitte, Ausdrücke mit every jedoch am Satzende.**
It'*s* always dark. We never *have* enough light. I meet Tony every day.

- **Adverbien der Art und Weise und des Ortes stehen meist am Satzende.**
He planned the crime carefully. I buy my vegetables at the market.

! **Bei mehreren Adverbien am Satzende gilt meist die Reihenfolge 1. Art und Weise, 2. Ort, 3. Zeit.**
Don gets **[Art und Weise:]** slowly **[Ort:]** out of bed **[Zeit:]** at six o'clock.

- **Gradadverbien stehen meist vor dem Bezugswort, jedoch hinter einem Verb (und dem Objekt).**
It's very *cold* here. I *like* Berlin a lot.

- **Satzadverbien stehen am Satzanfang, -ende oder in der -mitte.**
Perhaps Dave will come. / Dave will perhaps come. / Dave will come perhaps.

probably **und** certainly **stehen vor einem verneinten Hilfsverb:** I probably/certainly *won't come*.

Das Wichtigste in Kürze

- **Satzmitte: vor Vollverb, nach Hilfsverb, nach be – kein Adverb zwischen Verb und Objekt!**
- **Bei mehreren Adverbien am Satzende: Art und Weise – Ort – Zeit**

A One sentence has a mistake. Which sentence is correct?

a I go often to the cinema.
b I often go to the cinema. ✔

1 a I don't usually get much post.
b I don't get usually much post.

2 a We've always had a lot of pets.
b We've had always a lot of pets.

3 a We are still looking for a new flat.
b We are looking still for a new flat.

4 a Sue has every day lunch in the canteen.
b Sue has lunch in the canteen every day.

5 a Dave probably won't be on time.
b Dave won't be probably on time.

6 a We're going to London next month.
b We're going next month to London.

B Rewrite the sentences with the adverb in brackets in the correct position.

Bill spends his holidays in Italy. (usually)
Bill usually spends his holidays in Italy.

1 I'm busy. (often)

2 I won't be able to come tomorrow. (probably)

3 He speaks Spanish. (very well)

4 Jane and I meet. (every week)

5 I didn't go to work. (yesterday)

6 We've bought a small sailing boat. (just)

C Complete the dialogues by ticking the correct position for the adverbs in brackets.

A: Where do [ ] you [✔] spend Christmas? (usually)
B: We go [ ] to my parents' [✔]. (every year)

1 A: Do you go [ ] to your cottage in the country [ ]? (every weekend)
B: Normally yes, but we [ ] won't [ ] be able to go next weekend. (probably)

2 A: Have you [ ] got [ ] a headache? (still)
B: No, I took [ ] an aspirin [ ] and it's better now. (a couple of hours ago)

3 A: Do you [ ] buy [ ] your wine in France? (always)
B: No, there's a good wine shop in town. We buy it [ ] sometimes [ ]. (there)

4 A: Did you [ ] go to the bank [ ]? (yesterday)
B: No, I didn't have time. I'll [ ] go [ ] today. (in my lunch break)

5 A: What do [ ] you [ ] do in the summer? (normally)
B: We go [ ] to France [ ]. (every summer)

D Translate the following sentences.

1 Ich habe dieses Buch schon gelesen.
2 Ich fahre oft im Winter in Urlaub.
3 Mary fährt jede Woche nach Manchester.
4 Ich habe Tom gestern im Kino gesehen.
5 Wir werden vielleicht nächstes Jahr unsere Freunde in Amerika besuchen.

42 Nouns (1): non-countable nouns
Nomen (1): nichtzählbare Nomen

A: Do you want another ~~toast~~ piece of toast?
B: No thanks. I must get back to the computer.

A: Can you help me with my ~~homeworks~~ homework first? I need some ~~informations~~ information about Orson Welles.
B: Why don't you look on the Internet?

A: That's what I want to do, but can you give me ~~an advice~~ some advice where to look?

Zählbare Nomen – nichtzählbare Nomen

- Viele Nomen sind zählbar, z.B. book: a/one book, two books, three books.
  Manche Nomen sind nicht zählbar, z.B. weather: ~~a/one~~ weather, ~~two weathers~~, …
  Nichtzählbare Nomen haben keine Mehrzahlform und man kann kein a/an davorsetzen.

! Letzteres gilt auch, wenn ein Adjektiv vor dem Nomen steht.
What (~~What a~~) fantastic weather! *Was für ein tolles Wetter!*
You speak excellent (~~an excellent~~) German. *Sie sprechen ein ausgezeichnetes Deutsch.*
terrible traffic *ein furchtbarer Verkehr*, impossible behaviour *ein unmögliches Benehmen*
absolute chaos *ein absolutes Chaos*, lots of luck/stress *ein großes Glück / ein großer Stress*

Zählbar im Deutschen – nichtzählbar im Englischen

! Bestimmte Nomen, die im Deutschen zählbar sind, sind es im Englischen nicht.
That is useful information. (~~Those are useful informations.~~) *Das sind nützliche Informationen.*
Is this furniture new? (~~Are these furnitures new?~~) *Sind diese Möbel neu?*

advice *Rat, Ratschläge*	bread *Brot*	cloth, material *Stoff(e)*
help *Hilfe(n)*	toast *Toast*	furniture *Möbel*
information *Information(en)*	spaghetti *Spaghetti*	damage *Schaden, Schäden*
work *Arbeit(en)*	soap *Seife(nstück/e)*	knowledge *Wissen, Kenntnis(se)*
homework *Hausaufgabe(n)*	hair *Haar(e)*	progress *Fortschritt(e)*
housework *Hausarbeit(en)*	paper *Papier, Zettel*	proof *Beweis(e)*

- Vor einem nichtzählbaren Nomen kann some, any, a lot of, much stehen, nicht aber many.
  She gave me some important advice. *Sie gab mir wichtige Ratschläge.*
  The teacher didn't give us any homework. *Die Lehrerin gab uns keine Hausaufgaben.*
  We have a lot of information (~~many informations~~) now. *Wir haben jetzt viele Informationen.*
  How much proof is there? (~~How many proofs are there?~~) *Wie viele Beweise gibt es?*

- Als Ersatz für eine Einzahlform kann man vor advice, information, work, homework, bread, toast, soap, paper, cloth/material und furniture die Wendung a piece of verwenden.
  I need a piece of advice/information. *Ich brauche eine(n) Rat/Information.*

Das Wichtigste in Kürze

- Nichtzählbare Nomen: keine Mehrzahlform, keine Verwendung von a/an oder many
- Nichtzählbar im Englischen u.a.: advice, help, information, work, toast, bread, hair

A One sentence has a mistake. Which sentence is correct?

a This information is very interesting. ✔
b These informations are very interesting.

1 a Sue gave me some good advice.
b Sue gave me a good advice.

2 a Has all your new furniture arrived?
b Have all your new furnitures arrived?

3 a This is a really hard job.
b This is a really hard work.

4 a Can I have a toast, please?
b Can I have a piece of toast, please?

5 a What a wonderful music!
b What wonderful music!

6 a The storm did a lot of damage.
b The storm did a lot of damages.

B Correct any plural forms which are not possible.

We've just ordered a lot of new furnitures, for example two leather armchairs.

1 Although my son does a lot of homeworks, he doesn't seem to have made a lot of progresses this year.

2 My teacher at school always gave me useful advices. When I wanted to go abroad, she gave me a lot of informations about the various possibilities.

3 I have a lot of works at the moment. My boss always gives me more jobs to do than my colleague.

4 The police haven't made any progresses in the murder case. The public has given them a lot of helps and they have arrested two peoples but they still don't have any proofs that they are the murderers.

C Complete the following dialogues by underlining the correct forms.

A: I have such a lot of <u>work</u>/works at the moment.
B: Do you think you will finish <u>it</u>/them before your holiday?

1 A: Your hair look/looks nice.
B: Thanks. I had it/them cut yesterday.

2 A: I have a lot of homework/homeworks today.
B: Me, too. I have to write about Charles Dickens. I hope I can find some information/informations on the Internet.

3 A: Would you like another bread / another piece of bread?
B: No, thanks. Let's finish breakfast and go out. It's such a lovely weather / such lovely weather.

4 A: Sue speaks such good Italian / such a good Italian. Let's get her an Italian cookery book for her birthday.
B: I don't know. Her children say she only cooks spaghetti/spaghettis anyway.

D Translate the following sentences.

1 Haben sie genügend Beweise, dass er der Mörder ist?
2 Dieses Jahr haben Sie viele Fortschritte gemacht.
3 Sie kauft immer teure Stoffe.
4 Meine Haare sind viel zu lang.
5 Er spricht gut Französisch und seine Spanischkenntnisse sind nicht schlecht.

43 Nouns (2): singular and plural
Nomen (2): Einzahl und Mehrzahl

A: The news ~~are~~ *is* good – the weather in the Andes is good.
B: Great!
A: I bought ~~a new~~ *some new / a new pair of* sunglasses today. I paid over 150 ~~dollar~~ *dollars*.
B: Well, you have to protect your eyes up in the snow, don't you? Have you started packing?
A: Yes. You need so much for a ~~two weeks~~ *two-week* expedition – although two weeks ~~aren't~~ *isn't* really a long time.

Nomen, die es nur in der Mehrzahl gibt

! „Paarwörter" bezeichnen Dinge, die aus zwei gleichen Teilen bestehen. Diese gibt es im Englischen nur in der Mehrzahl.

I'm looking for some red jeans (~~a red jeans~~). *Ich suche eine rote Jeans.*
These jeans were (~~This jeans was~~) expensive. *Diese Jeans war teuer.*
Where are my glasses? (~~Where is my glasses?~~) *Wo ist meine Brille?*

Als Ersatz für eine Einzahlform kann man a pair of verwenden.
I need a clean pair of trousers / a pair of scissors. *Ich brauche eine frische Hose / eine Schere.*

glasses *Brille(n)*	pants *Unterhose(n)*	jeans *Jeans*
scissors *Schere(n)*	tights *Strumpfhose(n)*	trousers *Hose(n)*
binoculars *Fernglas/-gläser*	pyjamas *Pyjama*	shorts *Shorts*
headphones *Kopfhörer*		

! Auch police (*Polizei*), people (*Leute/Menschen*), stairs (*Treppe/n*), clothes (*Kleidung*), thanks (*Dank*), surroundings (*Umgebung*), outskirts (*Stadtrand*) gibt es nur in der Mehrzahl.

The police are (~~is~~) here. They are (~~It is~~) looking everywhere. *Die Polizei ist da. Sie sucht überall.*
These stairs are steep. *Diese Treppe ist steil.* Clothes are expensive. *Kleidung ist teuer.*

! Beachten: news und the United States stehen trotz der Endung -s mit einem Verb in der Einzahl.

The news is (~~are~~) good. *Die Nachrichten sind gut.*
The United States is (~~are~~) a rich country. *Die Vereinigten Staaten sind ein reiches Land.*

Mengenangaben mit Zahlen, Maßeinheiten, Währungen

! Maßeinheiten und Währungen haben – wie fast alle anderen Nomen – in der Mehrzahl ein -s.

ten kilometres *zehn Kilometer* six litres *sechs Liter* two pounds/dollars *zwei Pfund/Dollar*

Ein Verb folgt jedoch in der *Einzahl*, wenn ein Betrag, eine Menge oder Entfernung gemeint ist.
1000 dollars is (~~are~~) a lot of money. Three kilometres isn't (~~aren't~~) far. 70 years is (~~are~~) a long time.

! Wenn ein Nomen mit Zahl + Bindestrich vor einem anderen Nomen steht und diese Wendung die Funktion eines Adjektivs hat, entfällt das Mehrzahl-s.

an 18-hour day *ein 18-Stunden-Tag* a four-star hotel *ein Vier-Sterne-Hotel*

! Das Zahlwort million steht (wie hundred und thousand) nach einem anderen Zahlwort ohne -s.

6 million (~~millions~~) people *6 Millionen Menschen* ten million (~~millions~~) two hundred thousand

Das Wichtigste in Kürze

- Immer Mehrzahl: „Paarwörter", police, stairs, thanks, ... – aber nicht news, United States
- Maßeinheiten, Währungen mit -s (ten metres, six dollars) – Mengen jedoch + Einzahlverb (two hours is a long time); „Bindestrich-Adjektive" ohne -s: a four-star hotel

A One sentence has a mistake. Which sentence is correct?

a We stayed in a five-star hotel. ✔
b We stayed in a five-stars hotel.

1 a I've just had a bad news.
b I've just had some bad news.

2 a I need a new pair of sunglasses.
b I need a new sunglasses.

3 a She has a three years old son.
b She has a three-year-old son.

4 a Your pyjamas is on the bed.
b Your pyjamas are on the bed.

5 a I bought a ten-kilo bag of potatoes.
b I bought a ten-kilos bag of potatoes.

6 a The firm invested ten millions in the project.
b The firm invested ten million in the project.

B Singular or plural? Underline the correct form of the verb.

My shorts is/<u>are</u> dirty.

1 Your trousers is/are at the cleaners.

2 The news is/are on at 8 o'clock.

3 Ten kilometres is/are too far to walk.

4 Twenty-five minutes is/are a long time to wait for a bus!

5 The police has/have just come.

6 Those stairs is/are dangerous.

7 1000 euros is/are a lot of money.

8 Your new glasses looks/look great.

C Make complete questions.

Can your grandmother manage alone or *are* the stairs too steep?

1 Where .... clothes cheaper – in Germany or in England?

2 How much .... your new sunglasses?

3 I've got my discman but where .... my headphones?

4 What do you think – .... nine hundred dollars too much for this picture?

5 What size .... your jeans?

6 .... the scissors in the kitchen?

D Translate the following sentences.

1 Mehr als drei Millionen Menschen sind hier arbeitslos.
2 Die Vereinigten Staaten haben noch nie eine Präsidentin (*female president*) gehabt.
3 Die richtige Kleidung ist sehr wichtig für ein Vorstellungsgespräch (*interview*).
4 Ist das dein Fernglas?
5 Die Polizei ist in England nicht bewaffnet (*armed*).

44 some – any

A: I'm just going to the shop – we need ~~any~~ some more milk.
B: Can you get something for me, too?

A: What? I wasn't planning to go ~~somewhere~~ anywhere else, just to the shop for the milk.
B: I need some paper for my printer.

A: Sorry, but I don't really want to have to go into town. I've got hardly ~~some~~ any time this morning.
B: OK, I'll go myself. I'll get the milk too, if you like.

some und any in Aussagesätzen

- Vor nichtzählbaren Nomen (siehe Unit 42) bedeutet some „etwas", vor zählbaren Nomen in der Mehrzahl „einige / ein paar". Oft hat some jedoch keine direkte Entsprechung im Deutschen.

  We need some milk and some sugar. *Wir brauchen (etwas) Milch und (etwas) Zucker.*
  There are some biscuits in the cupboard. *Es sind (einige / ein paar) Kekse im Schrank.*

- not … any ist die Verneinung von some und bedeutet „kein(e)".

  There isn't any bread and we don't have any rolls. *… kein Brot … keine Brötchen.*

- some wird vor allem in bejahten Sätzen gebraucht, any (mit not) in verneinten.

  I'd like some salad. I don't want any bread.
  I have some dollars, but not any pounds.

  any wird auch in Sätzen ohne not verwendet, wenn die Aussage negativ ist.

  I'm too tired to do any more work. *… zu müde, um noch irgendwelche Arbeiten zu machen.*
  We have hardly any money. We never have any money. *… fast kein Geld / kaum Geld. … nie Geld.*

- any wird oft in if-Sätzen gebraucht.

  If there are any tickets, we could go to the theatre.
  If we have any time, we can visit Phil.

- any hat auch die Bedeutung „jede(r/s) (beliebige)".

  Any car costs money. *Jedes Auto kostet Geld.*
  Use any colour. *… jede beliebige Farbe.*

some und any in Fragen

- In Fragen wird meist any gebraucht.

  Have you got any money? *Hast du (etwas) Geld?*
  Are there any photos? *Gibt es Fotos?*

- some gebraucht man in Fragen, wenn man eine positive Antwort (yes) erwartet bzw. erhofft, insbesondere in Bitten und Angeboten.

  Can I have some water, please?
  Would you like some help?

someone/somebody, anyone/anybody usw.

- Für someone/somebody, something usw. gelten die gleichen Regeln wie oben.

someone/somebody	something	somewhere
(not) anyone/anybody	(not) anything	(not) anywhere

  Zwischen someone und somebody, anyone und anybody besteht kein Bedeutungsunterschied.

Das Wichtigste in Kürze

- some in bejahten Sätzen, any in verneinten
- Fragen: meist any; some in Bitten und Angeboten

A One sentence has a mistake. Which sentence is correct?

a Please buy any orange juice when you go shopping.
b Please buy some orange juice when you go shopping. ✔

1 **a** We need any more bread.
b We need some more bread.

2 **a** I haven't got anything to wear.
b I haven't got something to wear.

3 **a** Jane never has any time.
b Jane never has some time.

4 **a** I've got hardly any time this week.
b I've got hardly some time this week.

5 **a** This supermarket never has any fresh vegetables.
b This supermarket never has some fresh vegetables.

6 **a** I didn't see anyone I knew at the party.
b I didn't see someone I knew at the party.

B Underline the correct form.

Sue never has <u>any</u>/some money.

1 I'd like any/some grey jeans but I can't find any/some anywhere/somewhere.
2 Jane seems very upset about anything/something. I asked if I could help, but she wouldn't say anything/something.
3 Please buy any/some bread and any/some rolls but don't get any/some cake – there's still any/some left.
4 There was hardly anyone/someone at church this morning. I didn't see anyone/someone I knew.
5 I still haven't got anything/something for Jane's birthday. I want to give her anything/something for her new flat.

C Complete these dialogues with some/any, something/anything, someone/anyone or somewhere/anywhere.

1 A: Could you do .... for me, please?
B: Sure, but I don't have .... time this evening.

2 A: I've rung the office several times but I can't get hold of ....
B: There must be .... there.

3 A: I can't find my glasses ....
B: They must be here .... I think there's .... under the newspaper. Look there.

4 A: What time shall we meet tomorrow – .... time in the morning?
B: No, it will have to be in the afternoon because .... is coming to repair the heating in the morning.

5 A: I haven't done .... all day. It's been wonderful!
B: And I've been really busy. I haven't had .... time to relax.

D Translate the following sentences.

1 Gibt es irgendwo eine Telefonzelle?
2 Wir haben kaum Möbel in unserer neuen Wohnung.
3 Ich habe diese Woche keine Grammatik gelernt.
4 Wenn noch Käse im Kühlschrank ist, brauchst du keinen zu kaufen.
5 Ich habe seit zwei Monaten nichts von Susan gehört. Hast du etwas gehört?

45 much – many – a lot; each – every; most; none – nobody – nothing; enough

A: We've visited ~~the most~~ *most* places in the guidebook now.
B: Yes, but we haven't been on the river yet. I'd like to go on a boat trip.
A: OK. I think the boats go ~~all~~ *every* 30 minutes.
B: If we go now, we'll be able to get a boat at one o'clock.
A: We've got ~~time enough~~ *enough time*. Let's go and have a snack first.
B: Yes, OK. I'm feeling a bit hungry, too.

much – many – a lot (of)

- **much (*viel*) wird mit nichtzählbaren Nomen, many (*viele*) mit Mehrzahlnomen gebraucht.**
  There isn't much milk. How much butter is there? … *nicht viel Milch. Wie viel Butter …?*
  There aren't many men. How many women are there? … *nicht viele Männer. Wie viele Frauen …?*

- **much und many stehen meist nur in Fragen und verneinten Sätzen. In bejahten Sätzen steht meist a lot (of).**
  Is there much snow? No, there isn't much snow. There was a lot of snow yesterday.
  Can you see many people? No, I can't see many people. A lot of people have stayed at home.

each – every

- **each bedeutet „jede(r/s) einzeln für sich", every bedeutet „jede(r/s) von allen zusammen".**
  €50 isn't the price for five tickets. Each ticket costs €50! *Jede Karte [jede, einzeln für sich] …*
  I'm sorry, but every room is booked. … *jedes Zimmer [alle] …*
  Every single (~~Each single~~) room is booked. *Jedes einzelne Zimmer [restlos alle] …*

- **every entspricht „alle" in Häufigkeitsangaben.**
  A boat goes every three days / every 20 minutes. … *fährt alle drei Tage / alle 20 Minuten.*

! Nur each kann vor of stehen: Each (~~Every~~) of them is an expert. *Jede(r) von ihnen ist Experte.*

most

! **Vor der Mengenangabe most steht kein the.**
Most (~~The most~~) people would like to have a lot of money. *Die meisten Menschen [überhaupt] …*

Auf most kann of + the folgen, wenn von bestimmten Personen/Dingen gesprochen wird.
Most of the people here are new. *Die meisten [dieser bestimmten] Menschen …*

none – nobody – nothing

! **Nur none, nicht ~~nobody/nothing~~, steht vor of.**
None (~~Nobody~~) of my friends / of them knows. *Keiner/Niemand von meinen Freunden …*
None (~~Nothing~~) of the report / of it is true. *Nichts von dem Bericht …*

enough

- **enough steht hinter einem Adjektiv/Adverb, aber vor einem Nomen.**
  Tom is old enough. … *alt genug.* Ann has enough money (~~money enough~~). … *genug Geld.*

Das Wichtigste in Kürze

- much = „viel" – many = „viele"; in bejahten Sätzen aber meist a lot (of)
- each = „jede(r/s) einzeln für sich" – every = „jede(r/s) von allen zusammen"; vor of nur each
- Vor most kein the
- none (nicht ~~nobody/nothing~~) vor of
- enough steht vor einem Nomen

A One sentence has a mistake. Which sentence is correct?

a Nobody of my colleagues wanted to go to the Christmas party.
b None of my colleagues wanted to go to the Christmas party. ✔

1 **a** How much money do you have?
b How many money do you have?

2 **a** I know the most people at this party.
b I know most people at this party.

3 **a** The bus goes every 15 minutes.
b The bus goes all 15 minutes.

4 **a** Not much people live in this part of town.
b Not many people live in this part of town.

5 **a** No one of the students failed the exam.
b None of the students failed the exam.

6 **a** I don't have enough time to help you today.
b I don't have time enough to help you today.

B Answer these questions.

A: How often should I take these tablets?
B: (Alle vier Stunden) Every four hours.

1 A: Do all your colleagues speak English?
B: Yes, (die meisten) .... of them do.

2 A: How many of your friends smoke?
B: (Keiner) .... of them.

3 A: How often does the bus go to the airport?
B: There's one (alle zehn Minuten) ....

4 A: Are you busy?
B: Busy? I have (Arbeit genug) .... for a month!

5 A: How was the exam? Could you answer all the questions?
B: Yes, (die meisten Fragen) .... were easy.

6 A: Did you go to the concert?
B: Yes, there were (viele Menschen) .... there.

C Underline the correct answers.

Have you got <u>enough room</u> / room enough?

1 Did you see many police / much police at the demonstration?

2 I use my mobile phone a lot / much.

3 Sam won every match / each match last season.

4 We didn't have time enough / enough time to see everything in London, but we saw the most things / most things we wanted to see.

5 None of / Nobody of the tourists were satisfied with the hotel and there were a lot of / much complaints.

D Translate the following sentences.

1 Die meisten Leute hier sind aus Spanien.
2 Niemand von uns hat die Hausaufgabe verstanden.
3 Ich gehe alle zwei Monate zum Friseur.
4 Sie können Ihre Tasche hier lassen. Ich habe Platz genug.
5 Sie weiß viel über Politik.

46 all – everybody – everything; both – the two – either – neither

A: Have you met Tom's ~~both~~ two children?
B: No, I haven't. His daughter is very musical, a singer, isn't she?
A: Yes, everybody ~~say~~ says she's very good.
B: Have you ever heard her?
A: No, but ~~we're going all~~ we're all going to a concert next month where she's singing. Do you want to come?
B: When is it?

all – everybody – everything

! **Das deutsche „alle" (Pronomen) kann man normalerweise nicht mit all allein wiedergeben.**
Everybody sang "Happy Birthday". I knew everybody. *Alle ... alle [jedermann]*
Ed invited ***20 people***. Everybody / All of them came. *Alle [im Rückbezug auf genannte Personen]*
I tried ***six salads***. All of them were lovely. *Alle [im Rückbezug auf genannte Dinge]*

everybody/everyone **steht mit einem Verb in der Einzahl:** Everybody likes Tom. *Alle mögen Tom.*

! **Das deutsche „alles" entspricht all nur in der Bedeutung „das Einzige(, was)" (mit Relativsatz).**
All (that) I know is the date. *Alles, was [das Einzige, was] ich weiß, ist das Datum.*
Everything is so expensive. *Alles [alle Dinge / das Ganze] ist so teuer.*
Anything can happen at Ed's parties! *Alles [alles Mögliche] kann ... passieren.*
I'll do anything to help you. *Ich mache alles [irgendetwas, egal was], um dir zu helfen.*

both – the two – either – neither

- **both entspricht „(alle) beide". Mit both betont man: „nicht nur der eine, sondern auch der andere". Unbetontes „beide" entspricht the two.**
  The parents are divorced and the two children live with their father. *... die beiden/zwei Kinder ...*
  Aber: Both children live with the father, not just the son. *Beide /Alle beide Kinder ...*
  Do you know the two (people) by the door? *... die beiden ...*
  Aber: Do you know them both, or only the man? *... sie beide [alle beide] ...*

- **„beide" entspricht auch either und neither.**
  Which one would you like? You can have either (map). *... beide Karten [die eine oder die andere].*
  I'm afraid neither (map) is very up to date. *... keine von beiden [weder die eine noch die andere] ...*

Die Stellung von all und both

- **all und both stehen (wahlweise mit of) vor Wörtern wie my/these.**
  All (of) our rooms have a view of the sea. Both (of) those maps are new.

! **all steht mit the, wenn bestimmte Personen/Dinge gemeint sind; both steht mit oder ohne the.**
All children play. [generell] All the children (~~All children~~) are outside. They're playing in the park.
Both / Both the / Both of the children are outside. [**Aber** nicht: ~~The both children~~]

! **all und both stehen (als nachgestellter Teil des Subjekts in der Satzmitte) vor einem Vollverb, hinter einem Hilfsverb sowie hinter be (vgl. Unit 41).**
They all smoke / They are all smoking. (~~They smoke all / are smoking all.~~) *Sie rauchen alle.*
The ladies both drank / were both drinking tea. (~~drank both / were drinking both~~) *... tranken beide Tee.*

Das Wichtigste in Kürze

- „alles" und „alle" (Pronomen) = meist everything und everybody (nicht ~~all~~ allein)
- „beide" = both, wenn betont („nicht nur, sondern auch"), sonst the two (oder either/neither)
- Stellung *vor* einem Vollverb; all steht mit the, wenn bestimmte Personen/Dinge gemeint sind

A One sentence has a mistake. Which sentence is correct?

a Both my sisters are older than me. ✔
b My both sisters are older than me.

1 a Do you know my two colleagues?
b Do you know my both colleagues?

2 a All my friends are on holiday.
b All friends are on holiday.

3 a My cousins all came to my wedding.
b My cousins came all to my wedding.

4 a All is so complicated.
b Everything is so complicated.

5 a Everybody is here.
b Everybody are here.

6 a We both need a holiday.
b We need both a holiday.

B Cross out any articles which are not necessary.

I like ~~the~~ both pullovers but I'm not sure about the jeans.

1 I know all the people in this room.

2 Do all the German children start school when they are six?

3 The drivers were OK, but the both cars were badly damaged in the accident.

4 All the children from my son's class visited him in hospital.

5 I've read all the books by this author.

6 The boy is good at languages and the both girls are too.

C Add all or both to the following sentences.

The children are playing in the garden. (all)
The children are all playing in the garden.

1 My brothers live abroad. (both)

....

2 We work really hard in our office. (all)

....

3 We left the building when the fire alarm rang. (all)

....

4 My sister and I moved last year. (both)

....

5 We've passed the exam. (all)

....

6 My mother and father have problems with their health. (both)

....

D Translate the following sentences.

1 Ich würde alles tun, um ihn kennenzulernen. (kennenlernen = *meet*)
2 Meine beiden Nachbarn sind sehr freundlich.
3 Meine Freunde wollten alle helfen. Alle kamen.
4 Wir haben beide letztes Jahr ein neues Auto gekauft.
5 Welchen Koffer willst du? Du kannst beide haben – den roten oder den schwarzen.

47 The definite article "the"
Der bestimmte Artikel „the"

A: Are you going ~~to the church~~ to church this morning?
B: No, I haven't got time. The Webbers are coming. Have you forgotten? I've got to cook.
A: Can I help? What are we having ~~for the lunch~~ for lunch?
B: It will be easier if you let me do it on my own.
A: Perhaps I can sit and ~~play guitar~~ play the guitar – to relax you.
B: No, thank you. You go to church – and take the children with you!

Das Weglassen von the bei abstrakten Nomen

! **In allgemeinen Aussagen stehen abstrakte und Mehrzahlnomen ohne the.**

(~~The~~) Life is wonderful. *Das Leben* — (~~The~~) Love costs nothing. *Die Liebe*
(~~The~~) History can teach us a lot. *Die Geschichte* — (~~The~~) Nature knows best. *Die Natur*
(~~The~~) People are animals. *Die Menschen* — When did humans discover (~~the~~) fire? *Das Feuer*

! **Dies gilt auch, wenn vor dem Nomen ein Adjektiv oder nach dem Nomen eine Fügung mit einer Präposition steht.**

What do you know about (~~the~~) American history? — (~~The~~) Life in the Middle Ages was hard.

Wenn jedoch die Präposition of heißt, oder ein Relativsatz folgt, kann man the nicht weglassen.

The life of many in the Middle Ages was hard. — The life (that) I'd like to live is impossible.

Das Weglassen von the bei school, college, university, church, hospital, prison

- **Wenn man an den Zweck dieser Einrichtungen denkt (nicht an das Gebäude/Bauwerk) und von deren Nutzern spricht (Schülern/Studenten/Kirchgängern/Patienten/Gefangenen), entfällt the.**
  School finishes at 3.30. *Die Schule ist ... aus.* — **Aber:** Turn left at the school.
  Church starts at 9.30 today. *Der Gottesdienst* — **Aber:** The church was built in 1560.
  Tom goes to university soon. *auf die Universität* — **Aber:** Ann's a professor at the university.
  Ed will be in hospital for a week. *im Krankenhaus* — **Aber:** Sally is a nurse at the hospital.
  A terrorist escaped from prison. *aus dem Gefängnis* — **Aber:** The police are at the prison now.

- **the entfällt auch bei bed und town (in Verbindung mit Schlafen/Erledigungen), home und work.**
  When did he go to bed last night? Is he still in bed? — **Aber:** There's a spider (Spinne) in the bed.
  Is Tom still in town? I need to go (in)to town, too. — **Aber:** There are six churches in the town.

Das Weglassen von the bei Eigennamen, Mahlzeiten, Verkehrsmitteln

- **Im Gegensatz zum deutschen Sprachgebrauch entfällt der Artikel vor:**

– **Eigennamen der meisten Straßen, Plätze, Brücken und Parks und vieler Gebäude:**
We met in (~~in the~~) Park Street / at (~~at the~~) London Airport / near (~~near the~~) Victoria Station.
– **Eigennamen von Wochentagen und Monaten:** We met on Monday / in May.
– **Eigennamen von Seen und Bergen (nicht Gebirgen):** Lake Constance / Mount Everest is big.
– **Eigennamen, denen ein Adjektiv vorausgeht:** dear old Don, silly Joe, modern America
– **Mahlzeiten:** When's lunch? Let's talk after lunch. *... das Mittagessen? ... nach dem Mittagessen.*
– **by + Verkehrsmittel:** I came by car/bus/train/plane. (**Aber:** take the bus/train)

Bei Musikinstrumenten wird der Artikel dagegen gebraucht.
How long have you been playing/learning/teaching the guitar?

Das Wichtigste in Kürze

- **the entfällt: vor abstrakten Nomen (außer wenn of / Relativsatz folgt); oft vor Namen von Einrichtungen wie school, church; vor Eigennamen und Mahlzeiten**

Zu amerikanischem Gebrauch siehe Seite 103

A One sentence has a mistake. Which sentence is correct?

a We're having fish for lunch. ✔
b We're having fish for the lunch.

1 a In Britain children start the school at five.
b In Britain children start school at five.

2 a The violence has increased in recent years.
b Violence has increased in recent years.

3 a I usually get to work at 8 o'clock.
b I usually get to the work at 8 o'clock.

4 a It's time to go to the bed.
b It's time to go to bed.

5 a Life is not always easy.
b The life is not always easy.

6 a The Tower Bridge was closed for repairs.
b Tower Bridge was closed for repairs.

B Cross out any articles which are incorrect.

~~The~~ old people often need help. I often go shopping for the two old ladies next door.

1 I didn't go to the work yesterday. I stayed in the bed because I didn't feel well.

2 The children in my daughter's class are collecting money for the local church.

3 My grandfather is in the hospital at the moment. I can't visit him very often because the hospital is too far away.

4 My sister is studying at the Oxford University. She has a nice room near the university.

5 All the people in our village are against the new motorway. They are going to the Downing Street next week to hand in a petition.

6 The music is very important to me. I love the classical music and I play the piano.

C Underline the correct forms.

1 Last year we spent our holiday in the Turkey / Turkey. Our hotel was great – we had the breakfast / breakfast there and went to a restaurant for the dinner / dinner.

2 My son wants to go to the university / university in the United States / United States. Before he starts his course, he hopes to go to the Rocky Mountains / Rocky Mountains.

3 A lot of the people / people go to the Trafalgar Square / Trafalgar Square on New Year's Eve.

4 I visit my grandparents on Sundays. I usually go by the car / by car but if the weather is bad, I take the train / train. I take them out for the lunch / lunch.

5 The life / Life is very difficult for homeless people. Many of them need to go to the hospital / hospital but it is not always possible.

D Translate the following sentences.

1 Ist der Mont Blanc in der Schweiz?
2 Die britische Küche (*cuisine*) ist besser als die Leute meinen.
3 Ich liebe die Musik. Ich spiele jeden Tag Gitarre.
4 Ich nehme nie den Bus – ich fahre immer mit dem Auto zur Arbeit.
5 Mein Nachbar ist im Gefängnis. Das Leben dort ist hart.

48 The indefinite article "a/an"
Der unbestimmte Artikel „a/an“

A: Tamara's son speaks ~~such a~~ such good English now. I wish I had learned it ~~as~~ as a child.
B: Well, he's lucky. He has a very good teacher, and Tamara pays for extra lessons.
A: I know. How often are they? Once ~~in a~~ a week, twice ~~the~~ a week?
B: Nearly every day, because that's more effective. But the lessons are very short.
A: Twenty minutes, ~~a half~~ half an hour?
B: No, just fifteen minutes. It's very practical because the teacher lives in the same building.

Englisch: unbestimmter Artikel – Deutsch: kein Artikel

! Im Englischen steht manchmal der unbestimmte Artikel, wo im Deutschen kein Artikel nötig ist.

– Berufsangaben	Ann is **a doctor**. Her brother is **a teacher**.
– Nationalitätsangaben	Ed is **an Englishman**. (= Ed is English.)
– Angaben zu politischer/ religiöser Überzeugung	Sue is **a socialist**. Tom is **a Buddhist**.
– Angaben zu Genuss- und Sportgewohnheiten	Dave is **a smoker** / **a beer drinker**. Angela is **a jogger** and **a tennis player**.
– vor **member**, **expert**, **millionaire**, **optimist** und **pessimist**	Is she **a member** / **an expert** / **a millionaire**? Dad is always **an optimist** / **a pessimist**.
– vor **headache** und **cold**	I have **a headache** / **a cold**.
– nach **as**	**As a** child I hated fish.

a/an in der Bedeutung „pro“

! Nicht der bestimmte Artikel, sondern der unbestimmte Artikel wird in der Bedeutung „pro“ vor Zeit-, Maß- und Mengenangaben gebraucht.

I train **six times a week**. ... *sechs Mal die Woche.*
They cost **two euros a kilo**. ... *zwei Euro das Kilo.*

half, such, quite + a/an

! **a/an** steht hinter **half** und **such**, nicht davor.

I'll see you in **half an hour**. ... *in einer halben Stunde.*
It was **such a nice day**. ... *so ein schöner Tag.*

Achtung: Vor einem (Adjektiv +) Nomen kann **so** nicht stehen.
He's **such** (~~so~~) **an idiot**. He's **such** (~~so~~) **a stupid man**.

- Auch bei **quite** steht **a/an** in aller Regel dahinter, nicht davor.
  We got **quite a** shock. ... *einen ziemlichen Schock.*
  It was **quite a** long journey. ... *eine ziemlich lange Reise.*

Kein a/an bei nichtzählbaren Nomen

! Vor einem nichtzählbaren Nomen kann **a/an** nicht stehen (siehe Unit 42).

What (~~What a~~) wonderful **weather**! *Was für ein wunderbares Wetter!*

Das Wichtigste in Kürze

- **a/an** nach **as** und bei Angaben zu Beruf, politischer/religiöser Überzeugung, Gewohnheiten
- **a/an** vor **member**, **expert**, **millionaire**, **optimist/pessimist**, **headache**, **cold**
- **a/an**, nicht ~~the~~, in der Bedeutung „pro“
- **a/an** hinter **half**, **such**, **quite** – nicht davor
- Kein **a/an** vor nichtzählbaren Nomen

A One sentence has a mistake. Which sentence is correct?

a My mother is a doctor. ✔
b My mother is doctor.

1 a I learn English once in a week.
b I learn English once a week.

2 a What a good advice!
b What good advice!

3 a Let's meet in half an hour.
b Let's meet in a half hour.

4 a My boss is a chain smoker.
b My boss is chain smoker.

5 a Bill is member of the swimming club.
b Bill is a member of the swimming club.

6 a We gave her money as present.
b We gave her money as a present.

B Underline the correct forms.

1 A: It's such a lovely day / so a lovely day! Let's walk round the lake.
B: It's such a long way / so a long way. It'll take us at least a half hour / half an hour to get there.

2 A: Is your husband still member / a member of the rowing club?
B: Yes, he trains once in a week / once a week.

3 A: As student / As a student, I had a room with a strange family. The man was a drinker / drinker.
B: In my family the wife was alcoholic / an alcoholic and the husband was anarchist / an anarchist!

4 A: I'd like a half / half a pumpkin and how much are the mushrooms?
B: They're four euros a kilo / the kilo.

5 A: You're expert / an expert on Malta. Is this a good time of year to go there?
B: You know me – I'm optimist / an optimist. I went this time last year for three weeks and had such a good weather / such good weather.

C Make complete sentences and add any indefinite articles which are necessary.

Our neighbours have / such / beautiful garden. He's / professional gardener.
Our neighbours have such a beautiful garden. He's a professional gardener.

1 I got / such / shock when I heard about Sue's divorce. As / sales manager, she's away from home at least twice / month – perhaps that's the reason.

2 Tom is / such / idiot. He had / accident yesterday – he was driving over 120 kilometres / hour!

3 As / child, I had to help at home. My parents had / shop and worked six days / week.

4 Mary is / atheist and her husband is / strict Muslim.

5 We got / real surprise yesterday. Our daughter, who is / student in America, came home for my birthday. It's / half / year since we last saw her.

6 I've got / terrible headache. I think I'm getting / cold. It's not surprising – we've had / such / awful weather recently.

D Translate the following sentences.

1 Ich habe Kopfschmerzen. – Du arbeitest zu viel: 50 Stunden in der Woche.
2 Gestern hatten wir so ein herrliches Wetter. Der Tag war so schön!
3 Als Rentnerin (*pensioner*) ist meine Mutter nie zu Hause!
4 Ich habe so eine gute Ärztin. Ihr Mann ist auch Arzt.
5 Meine Kusine hat einen Engländer geheiratet. Er spricht ein gutes Deutsch.

Notizen

Grammatikalische Besonderheiten im amerikanischen Englisch

Der Sprachgebrauch im amerikanischen Englisch (AE) ist in einigen wenigen Punkten anders als im britischen Englisch (BE).

Present Perfect – einfache Vergangenheit (Units 7, 8, 10)

- Im amerikanischen Englisch wird sowohl das Present Perfect als auch die einfache Vergangenheit gebraucht, wenn etwas berichtet wird, das Auswirkungen auf die Gegenwart hat. Der Gebrauch der einfachen Vergangenheit ist häufig in Verbindung mit *just, already, yet, ever* und *before*.

  AE: Sonia just **phoned**.
  BE: Sonia **has** just **phoned**.

  AE: **Did** Tom **come** home yet?
  BE: **Has** Tom **come** home yet?

  AE: Bill **broke** his leg, so he can't drive us.
  BE: Bill **has broken** his leg, so he can't drive us.

- Das Partizip Perfekt des Verbs *get* lautet im amerikanischen Englisch *gotten*.
  AE: He**'s gotten** much fatter since I last saw him.
  BE: He**'s got** much fatter since I last saw him.

mustn't – needn't (Unit 24)

- Im amerikanischen Englisch ist *needn't* eher selten. Stattdessen wird (neben *don't have to*) *don't need to* gebraucht.

  AE: I **don't have to / don't need to** leave before 9.30.
  BE: I **needn't / don't have to / don't need to** leave before 9.30.

Der bestimmte Artikel „the" (Unit 47)

- *university* und *hospital* werden im amerikanischen Englisch mit *the* gebraucht, auch wenn man an den Zweck der Einrichtung denkt und von deren Nutzern spricht.

  AE: My father was **in the hospital** for two weeks last year.
  BE: My father was **in hospital** for two weeks last year.

- Eigennamen von (einheimischen) Brücken stehen im amerikanischen Englisch mit *the*.
  AE: This is a photo of **the Brooklyn Bridge**.
  BE: This is a photo of **London Bridge**.

- Bei Musikinstrumenten wird der Artikel im amerikanischen Englisch manchmal – wie im Deutschen – weggelassen.
  AE: Don plays **piano**.
  BE: Don plays **the piano**.

Index A -Z

Hier finden Sie eine Liste mit grammatikalischen Begriffen in Deutsch und Englisch. Diese Liste geht über das Inhaltsverzeichnis hinaus, weil sie alle Seiten aufführt, auf denen eine Struktur behandelt wird. Außerdem finden Sie Verweise auf einzelne Wörter, sowohl im Englischen, wie auch im Deutschen.

Wenn Sie sich also z.B. erinnern, dass man das deutsche *viel/viele* im Englischen unterschiedlich ausdrückt, aber nicht genau wissen, unter welcher englischen Struktur Sie nachschlagen sollen, so hilft Ihnen dieser Index, denn *viel/viele* ist wie auch z.B. *man* oder *dass* im Index aufgeführt. Vielleicht erinnern Sie sich auch, dass es im Englischen bestimmte Nomen gibt, die nicht im Plural stehen können. Gehört z.B. *advice* dazu? Ein Blick in diesen Index hilft Ihnen weiter.

Damit man auf einen Blick erkennen kann, ob es sich bei den aufgeführten Begriffen um Strukturen oder Einzelwörter handelt, sind die Wörter ***fett kursiv*** gedruckt, wenn es sich um deutsche Bezeichnungen für Strukturen und **fett** gedruckt, wenn es sich um englische Bezeichnungen für Strukturen handelt. Englische Stichwörter sind normal gedruckt und deutsche Stichwörter *kursiv*. Die Zahlen verweisen jeweils auf die Seitenzahlen im Buch.

Auf der Seite 110 finden Sie eine Gegenüberstellung von englischen und deutschen Begriffen, die in diesem Index verwendet werden.

A

B

O

P

Q

R

Englische Grammatikbegriffe und ihre deutschen Übersetzungen

active	*Aktiv, Tatform*
adjective	*Adjektiv, Eigenschaftswort*
comparison of adjectives	*Steigerung der Adjektive*
adverb	*Adverb, Umstandswort*
adverb of frequency	*Adverb der Häufigkeit*
comparison of adverbs	*Steigerung der Adverbien*
position of adverbs	*Stellung der Adverbien*
answer	*Antwort*
short answer	*Kurzantwort*
article	*Artikel, Geschlechtswort*
definite article	*bestimmter Arikel*
indefinite article	*unbestimmter Arikel*
backshifting of tenses	*Zeitenverschiebung bei der indirekten Rede*
comma	*Komma*
conditional	*Konditional*
conditional sentence	*Konditionalsatz*
continuous form	*Verlaufsform*
clause	*Teilsatz*
contact clause	*Relativsatz ohne Relativpronomen*
relative clause	*Relativsatz*
future	*Futur, Zukunft*
future continuous/ progressive	*Verlaufsform des Futurs*
future perfect	*vollendete Zukunft*
gerund	*Gerundium*
if-sentences	*If-Sätze*
indirect speech	*indirekte Rede, berichtete Rede*
infinitive	*Infinitiv, Grundform*
passive infinitive	*Infinitivform des Passivs*
-ing form	*-ing-Form*
negation	*Verneinung*
noun	*Nomen, Substantiv, Hauptwort*
abstract noun	*abstraktes Nomen*
countable noun	*zählbares Nomen*
plural noun	*Pluralnomen*
singular noun	*Singularnomen*
uncountable noun	*nichtzählbares Nomen*
object	*Objekt, Satzergänzung*
direct object	*direktes Objekt*
indirect object	*indirektes Objekt*
participle	*Partizip*
past participle	*Partizip Perfekt*
passive	*Passiv, Leideform*
passive continuous/ progressive	*Verlaufsform des Passivs*
past	*Vergangenheit*
past continuous/ progressive	*Verlaufsform der Vergangenheit*
past perfect	*Past Perfect, Vorvergangenheit*
simple past	*einfache Vergangenheit*
preposition	*Präposition, Verhältniswort*
present	*Gegenwart*
present continuous/ progressive	*Verlaufsform der Gegenwart*
present perfect	*Present Perfect, Perfekt*
simple present	*einfache Gegenwart*
progressive form	*Verlaufsform*
pronoun	*Pronomen, Fürwort*
emphatic pronoun	*emphatisches Pronomen*
reflexive pronoun	*Reflexivpronomen*
relative pronoun	*Relativpronomen*
proper names	*Eigennamen*
quantities	*Mengenbezeichnungen*
question	*Frage*
question tag	*Frageanhängsel*
question word	*Fragewort*
relative clause	*Relativsatz*
non-restricted relative clause	*nicht bestimmender Relativsatz*
restricted relative clause	*bestimmender Relativsatz*
reported speech	*indirekte Rede, berichtete Rede*
subject	*Subjekt, Satzgegenstand*
verb	*Verb, Tätigkeitswort*
irregular verb	*unregelmäßiges Verb*
modal verb	*Modalverb*
regular verb	*regelmäßiges Verb*
reflexive verb	*reflexives Verb*

Schreibbesonderheiten

Die Schreibweise eines Wortes kann sich abhängig von der anzuhängenden Endung ändern.

Endung -s wird zu -es (Unit 1)

- Endet ein Wort auf *-s*, *-ss*, *-sh*, *-ch* oder *-x*, so wird vor der Endung *-s* ein zusätzliches *e* eingesetzt.
  kiss ⇢ kiss**es**, wash ⇢ wash**es**, watch ⇢ watch**es**, fix ⇢ fix**es**

Stummes -e entfällt (Units 2, 5, 6, 7, 26, 40)

- Endet ein Wort auf stummes *-e*, so entfällt *-e* vor den Endungen *-ing*, *-ed*, *-er*/*-est*.
  make ⇢ **making**, hope ⇢ **hoping**, use ⇢ **using**
  hope ⇢ **hoped**, use ⇢ **used**, smoke ⇢ **smoked**
  white ⇢ **whiter/whitest**, wide ⇢ **wider/widest**

Verdoppelung von Endkonsonanten (Units 2, 5, 6, 7, 26, 40)

- Endet ein Wort auf einen (einzelnen) Vokal + einen (einzelnen) Konsonanten, so wird der Konsonant vor den Endungen *-ing*, *-ed*, *er*/*-est* verdoppelt, wenn:
  – das Wort nur eine Silbe hat.
  plan ⇢ **planning**, stop ⇢ **stopping**
  plan ⇢ **planned**, stop ⇢ **stopped**
  big ⇢ **bigger/biggest**, hot ⇢ **hotter/hottest**
  Ausnahme: Vokal + *w*/*y*/*x*:
  blow ⇢ **blowing**, pay ⇢ **paying**, fix ⇢ **fixing**
  low ⇢ **lower/lowest**, stay ⇢ **stayed**, fax ⇢ **faxed**

  – das Wort mehrsilbig ist und die Betonung auf der letzten Silbe liegt.
  beGIN ⇢ beGINNing, forGET ⇢ forGETTing, conTROL ⇢ conTROLLing
  preFER ⇢ preFERRed, conTROL ⇢ conTROLLed
  Ausnahme im britschen Englisch:
  travel ⇢ **travelling**, **travelled** (trotz Betonung auf der ersten Silbe)

-y wird zu -i (Units 1, 5, 7, 39, 40)

- Endet ein Wort auf einen Konsonanten + *-y*, so wird *-y* zu *-i* vor den Endungen *-s*, *-ed*, *-er*/*-est*, *-ly* (nicht aber vor *-ing*).
  hurry ⇢ **hurries**, try ⇢ **tries**
  hurry ⇢ **hurried**, try ⇢ **tried**
  busy ⇢ **busily**, easy ⇢ **easily**, lucky ⇢ **luckily**
  dry ⇢ **drier/driest**, easy ⇢ **easier/easiest**

-le entfällt vor -ly (Unit 39)

- Endet ein Adjektiv auf *-le*, so entfällt *-le* vor *-ly*.
  probable ⇢ **probably**, simple ⇢ **simply**

-ic wird zu -ical vor -ly (Unit 39)

- Endet ein Adjektiv auf *-ic*, so wird *-ic* + *-ly* zu *-ically*.
  tragic ⇢ **tragically**, automatic ⇢ **automatically**